A Treatise of the Loves of Christ to His Spouse
by Samuel Bolton
with chapters by C. Matthew McMahon

Copyright Information

A Treatise of the Loves of Christ to His Spouse, by Samuel Bolton, with chapters by C. Matthew McMahon Edited by Therese B. McMahon

Copyright ©2020 by Puritan Publications and A Puritan's Mind

Some language and grammar have been updated from the original manuscript. Any change in wording or punctuation has not changed the intent or meaning of the original author(s), and has been made to aid the modern reader.

Published by Puritan Publications
A Ministry of A Puritan's Mind ®
Crossville, TN
www.puritanpublications.com
www.apuritansmind.com

All rights reserved. No part of this publication may be reproduced, stored in a retrieval system or transmitted in any form by any means, electronic, mechanical, photocopy, recording or otherwise, without the prior permission of the publisher, except as provided by USA copyright law.

Manufactured in the United States of America

eISBN: 978-1-62663-384-1
ISBN: 978-1-62663-385-8

Table of Contents

Introduction to the Work 4

Meet Samuel Bolton 7

Part 1: The Text Explained 10

Part 2: Doctrines from the Text 15

Part 3: Christ's in Four Ways 30

Part 4: General Application 41

Part 5: Particular Application 55

Part 6: Use of Examination 70

Part 7: Use of Exhortation 92

Other Helpful Works 107

Introduction to the Work
by C. Matthew McMahon, Ph.D., Th.D.

This work by Bolton is a divine encouragement to the needy Christian soul, and a means of drawing in the unbelieving soul to the love of Jesus Christ. His text is Song of Songs 4:9, "Thou hast ravished my heart, my sister, my spouse: thou hast ravished my heart with one of thine eyes; with one chain about thy neck." This text is something, as he says, which after we have been some while in heaven, we shall be able to understand. Certainly, no one can understand this text fully, except those who have the full enjoyments of Christ's love. Bolton looks to help cast us into its depth, and let it comprehend us. He is very successful in this endeavor.

His doctrine is that the heart of Jesus Christ is exceedingly taken with his church and people. In fact, as the text shows, Christ is *ravished by his bride*. This comes to be a refreshing encouragement as well as a sober and solemn call to consider this Christ who loves his people so much.

Bolton demonstrates that which so endears the heart of Christ to his church is that which *takes* the heart of Christ captive in his innermost desires. He is "taken" by the beauties and graces of his people. It does not matter, in this sense, how much grace or how little grace there is in a believer. Christ is taken with such grace, because it is Christ in them, and he placed that grace there to make them conformed to his own image.

A Treatise of the Loves of Christ to His Spouse

The least grace of his church greatly takes his heart and moves him towards an inexpressible love for them, that, as Bolton comments, would sink us down forever in our contemplation of it, being without words, and most astonishing. Is this the way that *you* think about Jesus Christ and his eye towards you? Is he captivated by you, ravished by you, and in turn, are you then ravished back?

If you are a Christian, you *need* to hear Bolton on this text, because it will take your mind off, as he says, the blackness of your thoughts. You droop and hang down your heads in contemplation of sin, hell, justice, judgment and other doctrines associated with your depravity in light of God's holiness. As Christians, we often do this too much to our detriment, and as a result, we will not own that portion which Christ has left us, nor that comfort which Christ tenders and speaks to us by and in the Gospel. We are his people, 1. By his choice. 2. By his purchase. 3. By God's donation. 4. By his covenant. And if he has done this for believers, what will Christ yet do *more* for his church and people, than what he has done? What a blessing his love is toward us in giving us all things for life and godliness, comfort and consolation!

At the same time Bolton is lifting up the oppressed Christian who needs to be cheered and revived by the ravishing love of Christ to the soul, he also deals with those who never have loved Christ, and shows them the path they need to walk in to be saved, converted and comforted by the love of the Savior and

Introduction

power of his Spirit. What does Christ do, or what can he suffer more than he has done and suffered to persuade the unbelieving heart of his love in the Gospel? He will open this up lucidly and precisely.

May you be blessed in seeing Christ more clearly in this invigorating, rejuvenating, spiritually energizing, restorative, and revitalizing work by this eminent Westminster Divine. It will raise your soul to gain you a further love of the Savior who loves his people so much that he came and died for them, gave them all things, and has them forever on his mind and heart, for he is ravished with them in expressible love.

In His Grace,
C. Matthew McMahon, Ph.D., Th.D.
From my study, September, 2020

Meet Samuel Bolton
by C. Matthew McMahon, Ph.D., Th.D.

Samuel Bolton, D.D. (1606-1654), divine and scholar, who has been wrongly identified both with a son and a brother of Robert Bolton, B.D., was born in London in 1606, and educated at Christ's College, Cambridge.[1] In 1643 he was chosen one of the Westminster Assembly of divines. It is stated that he was successively minister of St. Martin's, Ludgate Street, of St. Saviour's, Southwark, and of St. Andrew's, Holborn. He was appointed, on the death of Dr. Bainbrigge in 1646, master of Christ's College, Cambridge, and served as vice-chancellor of the university in 1651. Although with "no ministerial charge" he "preached gratuitously every Lord's day for many

---

[1] Le Neve, *Fasti*, ed. Hanly, iii. 690, 607

years." It is believed that it was this Samuel Bolton who, in 1648, attended the Earl of Holland upon the scaffold.[2] He died, after a long illness on October 15, 1654. In his will he gave orders that he was to be "interred as a private Christian, and not with the outward pomp of a doctor; because he hoped to rise in the day of judgment and appear before God, not as a doctor, but as a humble Christian." Dr. Edmund Calamy preached his funeral sermon.

His works are rare. They are:
1. "A Tossed Ship making for a Safe Harbor; or a Word in Season to a Sinking Kingdom," 1644.
2. "A Vindication of the Rights of the Law and the Liberties of Grace," 1646.
3. "The Arraignment of Error," 1646.
4. "The Sinfulness of Sin," 1646.
5. "The Guard of the Tree of Life," 1647.
6. "The Wedding Garment," posthumously published.
7. "The Dead Saint speaking to Saints and Sinners," which is a series of works in one volume: (a) Sin The Greatest Evil, (b) A Treatise of the Loves of Christ To His Spouse,[3] (c) A Treatise of the Nature and Royalties of Faith, (d) A Treatise of the Slowness of Heart to Believe, (e) A Treatise of the Miserable Condition of Unbelievers, (f) A Treatise of the Wonderful Workings of God For His Church and People.

---

[2] Whitelocke, *Mem.* p. 387
[3] By Samuel Bolton, D.D. (London: Robert Ibbitson, 1656).

For Further Study:
Brook's *Puritans*, iii. 223-4; Clark's *Lives*, pt. i. 43-7; Calamy's *Funeral Sermon*, 1654; Bolton's *Genealogical and Biographical,* Abram's *Blackburn*, p. 264.

Part 1: The Text Explained

Song of Songs 4:9, "Thou hast ravished my heart, my sister, my spouse: thou hast ravished my heart with one of thine eyes; with one chain about thy neck."

This is a text, which after we have been some while in heaven, we shall be able to understand. No one is able to apprehend this text, but they who have the full enjoyments of this love. But things that are not possible to be expressed, are not totally to be omitted; and therefore, we will launch into the main ocean. And when we are not able to apprehend this love, let us cast ourselves in, and let it comprehend us.

Some things in the general we premise. 1. For the author, or penman, was Solomon inspired by the Spirit of God.

2. For the title of the book; it is called the Song of Songs; or, *a most excellent song*. So, it is called this for the excellency and sublimity of its matter. The doubling of the words declares its excellency. As when the scripture speaks of base things; by doubling the words they are more debased; "And he said, Cursed be Canaan; a servant of servants shall he be unto his brethren," (Gen. 9:25). A servant of servants shall he be, that is, a vile slave. So when it speaks of good things by doubling the words, it declares the excellency of the thing. Deut. 10:17, "The Lord your God, is God of gods, and Lord of lords." So much for speaking to the title.

3. As concerning the matter; there is difference among interpreters. 1). Aben-Ezra a Jewish rabbi, thinks it to be a history of the church of God from Abraham to Christ. 2). Another thinks it to be a history of the church from Christ, to the freedom of the church by Constantine, a Roman emperor, who lived in the beginning of the fourth century. 3). Another makes it contain a prophetical history of the condition of the church from David to the end of the world. And divides the book into these two parts. The church 1]. Under the law. 2]. Under the gospel. (1). The church under the law, from David to the death of Christ, which is continued from the beginning of the book, to the sixth verse of the fourth chapter. [1]. As it was from David to the captivity; which he says, is contained in the first chapter, and the two first verses of the second chapter. [2]. As it was in the captivity, from the second verse of the second chapter, to the fifteenth verse of the second chapter. [3]. As it was after the captivity, until the death of Christ, the abrogation of the church under the law; which continues from the fifteenth verse of the second chapter, to the sixth verse of the fourth chapter. (2). And from that, to the end of the book is contained a history of the evangelical church, until Christ's second coming. Of this mind is Brightman.

But to leave this, we think (and with us goes the stream of orthodox interpreters) that the subject matter of this book is a parabolical history of the mutual loves between Christ and his church, set down under the persons of the bridegroom, and his bride. And in this way, much of the book in general is set down. We will now draw nearer to our text.

In the former chapter we read, how the church, the spouse of Christ, declares her exceeding love to Christ, and her high appreciations of him, with her earnest desire to enjoy him, whom her soul saw so precious, and that Christ might discover to her, how kindly he took her affection.

In this chapter he again enters into a singular commendation of the excellency of the church, declaring also his unfeigned love to her.

The whole chapter contains these parts. 1. A singular commendation of the church by Christ; which is set down allegorically from the first verse to the fifth, and from the tenth to the fourteenth verse. 2. A gracious profession of Christ's love to his church, from the fifth verse to the tenth. 3. The church's reply, with Christ's answer again to her, verses 15-17.

In the churches reply there is 1. A commendation of her head and husband, verse 15. And, 2. An earnest desire, of further communication of his Spirit, and communion with himself, verse 16.

In Christ's answer there is contained a promise of his gracious acceptation of such fruits as the church shall yield him, verse 17.

This verse which I have read to you is a branch of the second part, the gracious profession of Christ his love to his church, of which if I read no more than this verse, we see enough set down to astonish and amaze us all. "Thou hast ravished my heart, my sister, my spouse."[4] What wonder is there if the kingdom of heaven suffers violence, when the king of heaven himself suffers violence! Christ here speaks in the manner of a lover, whose heart is exceedingly ravished, and taken with the beauties, virtues, and graces of his spouse.

Give me leave to explain the words, and we will then come to the doctrine.

1. *Thou hast ravished.* What is meant by that? The expression is great, that the God of heaven should be so taken, even to ravishment with his church and people. And yet let me tell you, the word speaks more than any expression can utter.

The word in the Hebrew gives the following interpretations. 1. Aben-Ezra translates, *rapuisti animam meam,* thou hast taken away, thou hast stolen away my heart, my sister, my spouse.

2. Rabbi Solomon, *Traxisti animam meam ad te,* thou hast drawn my heart to thee.

3. *Talmudici prisci,* says, *Copulasti cor meum cum tuo,* thou hast coupled my heart to thee; thou hast one-ed my heart. This is as if he should say, "you have so joined me, as you and I have but one heart."

4. Another, *vulnerasti cor meum,* thou hast wounded my heart, my sister, my spouse.

5. The seventy in the LXX, they set down *excordiasti, eripuisti cor meum,* thou hast unhearted me;

---

[4] Quid mirum, si regnum caelorum vim patitur, *etc.*!

thou hast taken my heart from me. And here our translators, *thou hast ravished my heart*. All which laid together, they are mighty expressions, setting down, to great wonder and amazement, the exceeding love of Christ to the church. "Thou hast ravished, wounded, stolen away, drawn my heart to thee."

2. *My sister, my spouse*. We will join them both together. Both are spoken of the same person, the church of God, which Christ calls, אֲחֹתִי כַלָּה (Sol. 4:9). 1. Sister, because she is the daughter of his father in heaven, and fellow-heir of glory with Christ. 2. Spouse, because Christ had married himself to her.

3. *With one of thine eyes. With one chain of thy neck*. Not to engage in a sermon on these alone, 1. With one of thine eyes; with one chain, *i.e.* with thy graces, thy wisdom, and knowledge, thy faith, and other graces. This is as if he had said, I do not need to behold both your eyes. The beauty of one of them is so great, it takes my heart. And I need not to behold all your ornaments. Even one chain alone has taken my heart, and drawn my heart to you." Christ has a high account of the least of his people's graces.

In this way having explained the words, we come to the conclusions. *Thou hast ravished my heart*.

Part 2: Doctrines from the Text

DOCTRINE 1: That the heart of Jesus Christ is exceedingly taken with his church and people. *Thou hast ravished.*

DOCTRINE 2: That which so endears the heart of Christ to them, that which takes the heart of Christ, is the beauties and graces of his people.

DOCTRINE 3: The least grace of his church greatly takes the heart of Christ. *One eye, one chain.*

We think he cannot love us because we are so weak in grace. But it is his own grace, though never so weak, and he can love this. We will examine the first of these.

Doctrine 1: that the heart of Jesus Christ is exceedingly taken with his church and people. In the prosecution of this we will show:

1. What is meant by his heart being taken.

2. We will show that Christ's heart is in this way taken.

3. We will show on what grounds his heart is so much taken with his church, and so come to apply it.

For the first part, what is meant by *his heart being taken?* And here I must tell you in the entrance to thinking about this, that we cannot sufficiently express it. It is one of the highest expressions in the Scriptures towards his church, that the heart of Jesus Christ should be taken with his church.

An expression, which if we but let it lie on our spirit, the weight of it would sink us. Shall I say he dearly and entirely loves us. Nothing is too much to do, nothing is too great to suffer, nothing is too much to give to us, he exceedingly loves us.

Shall I say, his heart exceedingly delights in us, his soul exceedingly rejoices over us, above all the world.

Shall I say, we are exceedingly precious in his eyes, we are "choice in his esteem," (Isaiah 43:3-4). Such as he will give the world for, such as he will give himself for, if he can but gain us, he esteems he has riches enough, and reward enough for it.

Shall I say, his desires are towards us, he in a manner desires no more than us; shall I say he thinks that he is happy in the enjoyment of us. We are reward enough for all his pains, and all his labor.

Why, all this and more, the scripture says, and all this is yet short of this expression, *his heart is taken with us.*

This, the next particular will give us further insight into. 2. That the heart of Jesus Christ is exceedingly taken, I may demonstrate to you by diverse arguments.

That which the thoughts are taken up with it, that the heart must necessarily be taken with it. This is plain, for you know a man will busy his thoughts about that which he cares for. If you want to know what you love, see what things your thoughts are on. This is as if he had said, there can be no better character to discover what your hearts are taken with, than to examine what your thoughts are most taken up with; for what the thoughts are taken up with, the heart is taken with. Now the thoughts of Christ are exceedingly taken up with his church and people. We are ever on his thoughts. There has not been a moment from all eternity in which we have been out of the thoughts of Christ. Before the world was, we were on his thoughts, he thought on us to everlasting life, loved us with everlasting love.

After we had lost ourselves, we were then on his thoughts, when he interposed himself between God and us, to stop his wrath from us. Before we came into the world we were on his thoughts, witness all the scripture, in which are such expressions of his heart to us. After he came into the world, you see we were the whole of his thoughts, we lay ever on his heart; you see by his doings, sufferings, prayer for us. Read John chapter 14-17. See how his thoughts were taken up with us, when he was to leave us, what love he showed, what care he expressed to us, what earnest prayers he put up to God for us. Read John 17:9 to the end of the chapter. Yes, and what provision he made for us, he would not leave us comfortless, but sends his Spirit to comfort us, to guide us.

And now he is in heaven, are not his thoughts on us? Did he not tell us he went to prepare a place for us, he went to do our work, to intercede for us, to plead for us? The church of Christ is never a moment off from the thoughts of Christ, (Isa. 49:15-16). And therefore, his heart is exceedingly taken with his church.

That which a man affectionately and in great endearment loves, that the heart is much taken with, be it a husband, be it a wife, child, the world, whatever. Now Christ exceedingly loves his church, we are said to be the dearly beloved of his soul, (Jer. 12:7). And read here, he loves us beyond all expressions, God so loved the world, (John 3:16). So, Christ loves us beyond all conceptions, Eph. 3:19, for it is a love which passes knowledge. In the former verse the apostle went about to measure this love, height, depth, breadth, length. But he found his line too short, his measure would not reach, therefore he concludes it is a love beyond all knowledge.

A man may express much love, but he may conceive of more than he can express. Why this love of Christ is above all we can conceive, above knowledge. It is an infinite love. It is, I say, an infinite love, which is more than if I should lay all the bowels in the creature together, *etc.*

It is a greater love than all. Witness what is done, suffered, and yet love above all. And therefore, Christ's heart is exceedingly taken with his church and people.

That which a man causes his heart to be glad with, and which he rejoices over, he must necessarily be taken with. A man will not rejoice over the enjoyment of something he does not love. The rich fool rejoiced over his full barns, but it was because his heart was taken with his possessions.

Joy is a fruit of the heart being taken with anything; you rejoice in your riches, husbands, *etc.*, in the possession of whatever your heart loves. Now the heart of Jesus Christ exceedingly rejoices over his church and people; they are his by donation, God gave them to him; they are his by purchase, he laid down his life for them; if we lay down our life to compass a thing surely we rejoice in it.

We are his riches, we his treasure, his Ammies, Ruhama's, and Hephzibah's, his precious ones, his people, his spouse; and therefore, he must necessarily rejoice over us, (Isaiah 62:4-5). "Thou shalt be called Heph-zibah, for the Lord delighteth in thee." Yes, "as the bridegroom rejoiceth over the bride, so shall thy God rejoice over thee," (Zeph. 3:17). The Lord will rejoice over you with joy, he will rest in his love, he will joy over you with singing. And therefore, seeing Christ rejoices, *ergo* is the heart of Jesus Christ exceedingly taken, *etc.*

That which a man delights to converse with, that his heart is taken with. Now Christ delights exceedingly to converse with his saints, he loves to speak to them, and he loves to hear them speak to him, Song of Songs 2:14, "Oh my dove, let me see thy countenance, let me hear thy voice, for thy countenance is comely, and thy voice is sweet." When the disciples are talking of him, Christ joins himself to them. *Ergo* is the heart of Christ much taken.

When the two were going to Emmaus, Luke 24:15, Christ comes and joins with them, delights in their talk. "Then they that feared the LORD spake often one to another: and the LORD hearkened, and heard it, and a book of remembrance was written before him for them that feared the LORD, and that thought upon his name," (Malachi 3:16). When God's people were gathered together, the Lord hearkened and heard.

5. That which a man thinks nothing is too dear for, nothing too much to give for, to do for, or suffer for, that the heart must necessarily be taken with such things. But it was in this way with Christ to his church. 1. He suffered in his body, those spittings, buffetings, scourgings, *etc.*, that was dear to him, which he gave his heart-blood for.

2. He suffered in his soul even the wrath of God for her.

3. He emptied himself of his own glory, took on him the form of a servant, with all our infirmities; penal, not culpable, as it is said of Jacob, he counted all his labors but little for Rachel, because he loved her, (Gen. 29:20).

6. That which a man's soul is satisfied and contented with in its enjoyment, that is what a man's heart is taken with. If a man's heart were not taken with the love of a thing, he would never think himself happy, never be contented and satisfied with its enjoyment. Whereas on the contrary, where the soul is filled with

satisfaction in its enjoyment (whatever it is) the heart is taken with it.

Now you shall see that the heart of Jesus Christ is fully satisfied and contented with the enjoyment of his church, though it had cost him so much pains, so much sweat and blood, yet the enjoyment of it is reward enough to him. It is the reward which God promised him for his work, Psalm 2:8, "Ask of me, and I will give thee the heathen," *etc.* Here, merit of me, lay down your life, and I will then give you a church, a people. And that which satisfies, Isa. 53:11, "He shall see of the travail of his soul and be satisfied." What does this mean but that he shall see the fruit of his sufferings in the saving of souls, and shall be satisfied with it. It shall be reward enough to him for all pains that souls are saved. Isa. 62:11, "His reward is with him, and his work before him, he is the salvation of his people."

And this is that which some think is meant by the "joy set before him," in Heb. 12:2, "Who for the joy that was set before him, endured the cross, despised the shame." Which joy (a holy and learned interpreter says) is nothing else but the fruit of his sufferings, the redemption and salvation of his church and people, according to that in Isa. 53:12. "Therefore will the Lord divide him a portion with the great, and he shall divide the spoil with the strong, because he hath poured out his soul unto death." And it is an interpretation which may be backed.

Part 2: The Doctrines from the Text

Well then, seeing whatever the heart of man rests satisfied in its enjoyment, the heart is taken with it. And that Christ rests satisfied in the enjoyment of his church and people, though it cost so much to obtain it. *Ergo* it necessarily must follow that the heart of Jesus Christ is exceedingly taken with his people.

That which a man is exceedingly dear of, his heart must necessarily be taken with. Those things which take our hearts, we are exceedingly dear for them. If it is the world, husband, wife, child, a man is exceedingly excited for them. Deal gently with the young man Absalom, 2 Sam. 18:5, his heart was taken with him, and he was exceedingly taken with him.

Now Christ is exceedingly taken over his church. Oh! It is dear to him, therefore he gives charge to the world, do not touch one of these, for if you touch the apple of my eye, do not offend one of these little ones, for they are dear to me, he is taken with them and protective of them. Yes, he not only charges, but menaces too, and threatens men if they shall hurt any of his little ones. It had been better for you, that a millstone were tied about your necks, and cast into the middle of the sea, than to offend any of these little ones. Christ is exceedingly suspicious over his church and people for their good, for they are dear to him.

Take a taste of it in Job 18:8, "For he is cast into a net by his own feet, and he walketh upon a snare." When he himself was in that agony, and when he suffered himself to be hailed before the judges, and to die, yet you see how he was over his disciples; "why" Christ says, "I am he you seek for, if therefore you seek me, let these go their way." As if he had said, I am he whom you seek, and against whom your malice goes forth, do what you will with me, but spare these, let these go (what have these done?). With Jonah, "cast me into the sea, that the storm may cease;" nail me on the cross, fling me into the grave, do with me what you will, that these may escape.

Oh! Christ must necessarily be protective of them, when he would put his back between his church and the stripes, interpose his soul between the wrath of God and them. Drink of that bitter cup that they might not taste of it, be wounded that they might be healed, bear the curse, that they might carry away the blessing, as there was no sorrow to his sorrow, so no love to his love, all loves are lost, nay, seem hatred in comparison of his.

Another place, John 17:9-16. See there when he was to go from them, how protective he was over them. He commends them to his Father, and designs him *to keep them whom he had given him.* This is as if he had said, Father they are mine, and I love them dearly, I have done much for them, but I will do more, therefore preserve them, therefore keep them. I am no more in the world, but these are in the world, holy Father, through your own name keep those whom "thou hast given me;" in this way you see how concerned Christ was over them. And therefore, his heart is exceedingly taken with his church.

Part 2: The Doctrines from the Text

He will keep them from trouble, he will buy out their trouble with the troubles of the whole world, and their lives with the lives of thousands. You have a place for this in Isa. 43:3-4, "I gave Egypt for your ransom, I gave Ethiopia and Seba for thee." God will give whole kingdoms for his church to preserve them from trouble. "I have loved you, therefore will I give men for you, and people for your life." As if he had said, I stand at it to give the heads of a thousand men, the lives of ten thousands to save your life, to preserve you like the ram to save Isaac, he is protective and concerned with them; if not to keep them from trouble, yet to support them in trouble.

He is concerned of them, for he will deliver them out of trouble, and he will not suffer the rod of the wicked to rest. Though for a time, yet, *etc.,* many are the troubles of the righteous, but he knows how to deliver his, and reserve the wicked. If Christ does not deliver you from trouble, yet he will deliver you in trouble; and at last he will deliver you out, who knows how to deliver his. That which a man thinks everything else is too little, nothing is too much, noting is too dear to bestow on them, and so, *that heart* of a man is exceedingly taken with it.

Where all the expressions that a man can lay out, do still fall short of his affections to it, it is a sign the heart is much taken with such a thing. When a man does not think riches, nor labor, nor his blood, or his life is too dear, this shows the heart is much taken with it.

Now the church is so dear to Christ, that he thinks nothing too dear, nothing too much for it. It was not his blood within his veins, nor his life within his breast, which he counted too dear for her. He can seemingly bestow anything on her. He will bestow temporals on her, at least so much as is necessary for her. All things necessary for life and godliness, if he gives himself, how much more all things? (Rom. 8:32). Will he give the greater, and deny the less? No. That love which gave the greater, will not deny you the less; if it is good for you. So much so that he has engaged himself by covenant to give you as to bear your charge to heaven, and then there is nothing lacking for you at all. "The lions shall hunger and suffer want," *etc.* He bestows grace on you; and faith is more precious than gold. He might bestow outward things on you, and yet his heart never taken with you. The rich man Dives had more wealth, uttered more eloquence, Saul had more command, Agrippa had more glorious apparel, than those his heart is taken with. He may give wealth to a Dives, command to a Saul, eloquence to a Herod. But he never bestows grace on any, but it is an evidence his heart is taken with a man, as when Abraham gave portions to the sons of the concubines, but Isaac had the inheritance.

He will bestow his Spirit on you, to enlighten, renew, *etc.* He will bestow himself on you, the Collector of all other blessings. God cannot extend his love further in giving, nor we ours in desiring. And that which a man bestows himself on must necessarily be precious in his eyes. Christ bestows himself on you.

Who is the *summum genus* of gifts, the gift of gifts? The gift which entitles us to all other gifts, all is yours, if you are Christ's. The gift which sweetens and sanctifies all others, like the unicorn's horn takes away the venom and poison of all other. There is a curse with all other gifts if Christ is not given. A curse to your gold, your silver, your prosperity, your meat, drink, health, and strength. But where Christ is given, he takes off the curse, and sanctifies everything; he not only turns comforts into blessings, but crosses into blessings.

A blessing in sickness, in poverty, in death, *etc.* Christ bestows himself on his church, he passes over himself, and all his by his *deed of gift*, he and all his is yours: as you and all yours are his; your sins, and sorrows are all his.

And all his are yours; his merits, his Spirit. As Christ said to the Father, so may you say to Christ, "all yours is mine;" his merit is your clothing, his blood is your drink, his flesh is your meat. He is meat, drink, clothes. Christ does not stay here, but he bestows heaven on his church. It is the manor house which he has reserved for his spouse. "Father, I will that those whom thou hast given mee, may be where I am," *etc.* (John 17:24). They are married together, and co-habitation is a marriage duty, *etc.*, as Ahasuerus had two houses for his spouses.

And therefore, seeing Christ thinks nothing too dear to bestow on his church, here must necessarily follow; that the heart of Jesus Christ is exceedingly taken with his church.

1. Those which Christ has made all things for, to serve for the good of them.

2. Those whom he has prepared glory for, heaven for.

3. Those which he has shed his blood for, must necessarily be dear to him, his heart is much taken with them.

If a king should build a stately house, for one with whom he would solace himself all his life, and should at last give life too, you would think, surely, he loved him.

1. God made all for you, the sun, moon, stars, creatures; all this frame of the world; surely you are dear to him.

2. God prepared heaven for you, a place of glory, happiness; where you should forever enjoy him, and solace yourself with his love.

3. Christ shed his blood for you, which was more dear to him than ten thousand worlds. What is all the world, and ten thousand worlds in comparison of one drop of his blood? And therefore, they whom he shed his blood for, must necessarily be more dear to him than all the world; his heart is very much taken with them.

Part 2: The Doctrines from the Text

In this way we have looked at the rich cabinet of Christ's love, of which he has cheered and revived us. We will now proceed to the further discoveries of it, and that is, to the third thing we propounded, why the heart of Christ is so much taken with his church and people.

We will but give you these three grounds, all which are taken not from us, but from himself, from his own mercy. In brief, either it is from his own grace *to* us, or from his own grace *in* us.

The first ground or reason, why the heart of Christ is so taken, is, 1. Because we are his. Propriety you know is the great ground of love. We love our own; our own husbands, wives, children. They are ours; we have propriety in them. So here, we are his; he has propriety in us, and therefore, loves us. In Song of Songs 7:10, the spouse makes the same argument. "I am my beloveds, and he is mine," therefore his desire is towards me, therefore his heart is taken with me; therefore, his soul loves me. And we are his, in the dearest and sweetest relations.

1. We are his people, his subjects. Christ is the King of saints, whose throne is in our hearts, and will allow no rival. His scepter is his word, and whose word is our law. No, unless this amounts to too *little:*

2. We are his friends. "Henceforth I call you not servants, but friends." We are his friends and favorites. *No:*

3. We are his children, begotten again, and born again to everlasting life, (1 Peter 1:3-4). Being born again, *etc.*

4. We are his spouse, such as he has married to himself in faithfulness and truth, and such as he delights in.

5. We are his members. The church is his body, his fullness, and everyone are members in particular, as the apostle speaks.

6. We are his jewels, his treasure. Malachi 3:7, "In the day that I make up my jewels, they shall be mine." And therefore, his heart must necessarily be taken with us. Christ has the same argument. Where the treasure is; there will the heart be also. The heart, and a man's treasure lie together. Now, we are his jewels, his treasure, his portion, his inheritance; that which his Father left him; and he must dearly earn it too. And therefore, the heart of Christ is exceedingly taken with his church and people. So, you see this is the first ground, why, because we are his, and his in the dearest, nearest, choicest of relations.

Part 3: Christ's in Four Ways

His people are his, these four ways. We are his, 1. By choice. 2. By purchase. 3. By donation. 4. By covenant.

1. First, we are his by choice. He set his heart on us from everlasting, which was his first love, and that which has carried God through all the expressions of his mercy towards us, to this day, even to admiration of angels, and astonishment of men. These were his primitive, his heart-thoughts to us, his first love, which is most dear and precious. It is the first love of the creature to the Creator which is most precious in God's esteem. It is the virgin-love of the soul to God, those affections the soul has, when first enamored with God. Therefore, he tells the children of Israel, he remembered "the time of her espousals, the kindness of her youth." That will not go out of his mind, (Jer. 2:2).

So the first love of the Creator to the creature; his heart-thoughts, they are most precious. O! These take the heart; these are the fullest, these are his freest thoughts towards us, (2 Tim. 1:9). All the world stood before him, from the first man to the last. Why should he choose us, and pass by others? Others may be finer pieces of clay than we are. Others may be of greater parts, greater abilities, which if it had pleased God to have conquered to himself, might have brought him far more glory, done him more service. Here was only his free mercy. There was no ground to make him choose us, before he loved us. But there is some ground to cause him to love us, now that he has chosen us. We are his, and his by free choice, chosen and singled out of a world of men. And therefore, he will love us.

2. We are his by purchase. He has bought us, and that at a dear rate, with the price of his own blood, (Gal. 4:5). Christ was made under the law, that he might buy out those, who were under the law. Therefore, 1 Cor. 6:20, "You are bought with a price. And what was the price? It could not be too little for the meanness of the commodity, not worth owning when he had it. But it cost him his dearest heart's blood, as 1 Peter 1:18 says, that we "were not redeemed with corruptible things, as silver and gold, but with the precious blood of Christ, as of a lamb, without blemish, without spot." So, then, we are his by purchase; we are the fruits of all his pains; of all his doings and sufferings; we are the comings in which Christ had for his blood; we are his purchase.

God did covenant and bargain with Christ, that if he would lay down his life and blood for a people, he should have them. This you see in Psalm 2:8, "Ask of me, and I will give thee the heathen for thine inheritance," that is, one good preacher says, merit of me, lay down your life and blood, and you shall have a people, as you see in Isa. 53:11-12, "He shall see of the travail of his soul." That if he would die, we should live. If he would bear the curse, we should have the blessing. If he would bear that wrath our sins deserved, and interpose himself between the justice of God and us, the quarrel should be taken up; God would be at peace. If he would purchase us, he should enjoy us. And Christ undertook this. He loved us; and seeing he could not have us, except by buying us, and could not buy us, except he gave his blood for us, and as it were sell himself to the justice of God, that he might buy us out. He was content to do it. He redeemed us, not with silver or gold, *etc.* And now being purchased by him, his by purchase, and so dear a purchase, his heart must necessarily be taken with us. Indeed, he bought us, because he loved us: and now he loves us, because he has bought us. If we did lay down our blood, our life for the purchase of a thing, and could after live to enjoy it, how exceedingly would our hearts delight in it! Christ has given his blood, and laid down his life for the purchase of his church and people; and he lives to enjoy his purchase; and therefore, the heart of Christ must necessarily be taken with it.

Shall I tell you? You are all the delight which Christ has in the world. He delights to see you, he delights to be with you; he delights to converse with you; and all the delights of Christ are taken up with you; he has nothing worth beholding but you, in the world.

3. We are his by donation. God has given us to him, John 6:37, "All that the Father has given me, shall come unto me." John 17:9, 11-12, "I pray not for the world, but for them whom thou hast given me. Holy Father, keep through thy own name those whom thou hast given me."

We were so bought, as yet we were given. Otherwise, where is God's mercy? And so given, as yet we were bought. Otherwise, where is his justice? God's arms are equal; in the length of the one, you have the measure of the other. And therefore, he so expressed his mercy to man, as with it he preserved his justice. They were so given, as yet bought; and so bought as yet given. And being his by donation, God having given them over to Christ by deed of gift, being the full desire of Christ, we find that the heart of Christ is taken with them.

4. We are his by covenant, Ezek. 16:8, "Then I entered into covenant with thee, and thou becamest mine." Christ became ours; we became his. He is our king, and we his people. He is our husband, and we his spouse. He has given himself to us, and we have re-given ourselves to him. We are his delight, and he is ours. And being his in covenant, in mutual stipulation, and bargain, the heart of Christ is taken with us.

2. Because she is adorned with his beauties. She is beautiful, Song of Songs 4:1, 6:4, 10. There is a twofold beauty which Christ communicates to his church, which makes the church lovely in his eyes. 1. The beauties of his righteousness. 2. The beauties of his holiness and graces. But these are not communicated the same way. The one is communicated to us by imputation. The other by emanation, or infusion. The one a beauty, imparted. The other is imputed.

1. Christ communicates to his church his imputed beauty, then 2. His righteousness, which with he clothes our souls. Therefore, he is called Jehovah-our-righteousness, and is said to be made wisdom,

righteousness, sanctification and redemption. And we in this are to put on Christ.

Now this righteousness Christ communicates to us by imputation making it ours, is as if we in our own persons had worked it. And it is as truly ours to save us, to justify us, as it is his to glorify him. And God looking on us through Christ, and Christ looking on us in himself, as clothed with his righteousness, he beholds us as beautiful. He sees no iniquity in Jacob, nor transgression in Israel. Not that there was no iniquity in Jacob; but God did not see that iniquity as to count it against him; God looked on him as clothed with the righteousness of Christ, and so is said, not to see it.

As the sun shining through red glasses upon a wall, the wall looks red. Not that this color is inherent in it; but lucent on it. So God looking on us through Christ, beholds us righteous in his righteousness; not that this is inherent in us, or beheld in us; as the papists charge us, but *quoad gratiosum dei conspectum*, we are rather beheld in it.

I am not ignorant, there are some, besides papists, that deny the imputation of Christ's righteousness, and say too much with them, *justitiam Christi imputari commentum est*, and call this imputative righteousness, an imaginary and fancied righteousness. I wish they would consider what we say. We say there is a twofold righteousness in Christ. 1. His essential and personal righteousness, as God. 2. His mediatory righteousness, fashioned as Mediator.

The first of these cannot be imputed to us; it is essential, but the latter of these (*justitia mediatoria*) his mediatory righteousness, or that righteousness he fashioned for us as Mediator, by which he subjected himself to the precepts, to the penalties, commands, and curses; answering both God's vindictive and rewarding justice, this is communicated to us, and made ours, by virtue of which we stand *recti in curia*, justified in God's sight, which is the first beauty Christ adorns his church with.

2. A second beauty wherewith Christ adorns his church, and makes her lovely, is, the beauties of his graces; which may be called the beauties of holiness, and set forth to us by those bracelets, and chains.[5] And here by one chain, *etc.* Which is communicated to us, by way of infusion, or emanation, by which Christ by his Spirit, derives from himself as the universal principle, and common stock of grace, grace for grace, according to John 1:16, "Of his fulness we have all received grace for grace."

I know there are many interpretations of this. Chrysostom says this is the gospel for the law, because it follows, the law came by Moses. Others, *gratiam, super gratiam, or gratiam gratiae accumulatam*, one grace to another, or abundance of grace. But this I conceive the meaning to be. For every grace that is in Christ, there is some grace communicated to us

---

[5] "Then washed I thee with water; yea, I thoroughly washed away thy blood from thee, and I anointed thee with oil," (Ezek. 16:9).

answerable to it, in some proportion. As the child in generation receives from the parent's member for member; or as the paper from the press, letter for letter; or the glass from the face, image for image; or the wax from the seal, stamp for stamp, so we from Christ, grace for grace.

There is no grace in Christ appertaining to our sanctification in general, which is not in some weak degree fashioned in us. And here the work of grace and regeneration is called "a forming of Christ in the soul." And while we behold him, we are said to be changed into his likeness, (2 Cor. 3:18). And we are said to have the same Spirit in us, that is in Christ. Romans 8:9, "If any man have not the Spirit of Christ, he is none of his." And the same mind is in us, that is in Christ, (Phil. 2:6).

There is a bastardly holiness, a painted false beauty, which is spun out of ourselves, fashioned out of our own principles, with which we shall lie down with sorrow at last. Sparkles of our own kindling. But the true holiness flows from Christ, and is imparted from Christ to his church, by which she is beautiful with his beauties, adorned with his graces. And being in this way, the heart of Jesus Christ must necessarily be taken with her.

In this way, you see the second reason, why the heart of Christ is so much taken. Because she is adorned with his beauties, clothed with his righteousness, adorned and beautified with his graces; which engages the heart of Jesus Christ. He that loved us in our own blood, cannot choose but love us, as we have his beauty put on us; he cannot but love himself, and delight in himself, wherever he beholds himself. Why, these beauties are pieces of himself, part of his beauty, his rays with which he himself is adorned. And he cannot look on any soul clothed with his righteousness, and beautified with his graces, but his heart is exceedingly taken with them. Song 6:4-5, "Turn away thine eyes from me, for they have overcome me." Christ seems as not able to bear the view of such a beauty. Turn away thine eyes, *etc.*

2. Because they are the persons, on whom God intended to advance the great design of glorifying the riches and freeness of his grace and mercy.

Now those whom God has intended for so great purposes, as these are, which are the greatest purposes that ever came on his heart, so his heart must necessarily be taken with it. You know the more glorious and excellent the end to which anything serves, the more precious is that thing in our eyes. Now we serve for no other end, but the expression of his mercy, the advancement of the glory of his free-grace, which are ends as high as himself, purposes as great as himself.

And therefore, God is not only taken with its expression, but with the persons upon whom he expresses it. Therefore, I say is the heart of God so exceedingly taken with his church.

Indeed, God may single out some men for the purposes of expressing the glory of his power and justice, the advancement of them; and yet God hates the men, as you see it plain in Pharaoh, who for this cause was set up to advance his power. But God never singled out any to be the subjects on whom he intends to advance the riches of his grace and mercy; but his heart is exceedingly taken with them.

Those, who serve to such high purposes as these, and are designed to such high ends as these; the advancement of the glory of his grace and free-mercy (which is the most precious attribute of God, and which some think is called his glory, Exod. 33:18, "Let me see thy glory,") and if the 19th verse may interpret it, that glory was his mercy, and his mercy his glory; and therefore, such must necessarily be precious in his esteem.

Now his people are they, whom God has singled out for these great purposes, for the expression of more mercy, than we can express, no, than we can conceive, no, than we can believe at all times, but weakly at best. And therefore, the heart of Jesus Christ must necessarily be taken with them.

My brethren, if God had not singled out some to express himself on in this way, God would have not been known in the world; for there is nothing so much that reveals God to be God, as his mercy and grace. And therefore, God singled out a few on whom he would advance the riches of his grace, that his mercy, and in that himself might be made known in the world. As Paul says of himself, 1 Tim. 1:16, "That he obtained mercy, that he might stand up a pattern of all long-suffering." As if he had said. We should not have known how patient God is, we should not have apprehended how long-suffering God is to sinners, if he had not had such an example of patience, such a pattern of all long-suffering, as I was. So we should not have known how merciful, how good God is, if the choicest attribute of God had been lost to us; like as if a great river had run underground not discerned, if God had not singled out some, on whom he might have expressed the riches of his mercy.

And those whom God intends to be the subjects on whom he may advance so high designs, so great purposes, must necessarily be exceedingly precious to him.

My brethren, you that are the people of God, are such as he has intended to advance his mercy, and glory of free-grace on; you are they he sent Christ to die for, the greatest work that ever was fashioned in the world. You are they whom he reared the fabric of heaven for. You are they in whom he intends to delight, and with whom he will solace himself for ever.

And God looks on us now, not as we are, but what he intends to make us. He sees to the utmost of his design on you, to eternity, and loves you now with that love. If God should look on us, as we are, he might see enough in us, to withdraw his heart from us. Or if not, yet enough to cool and quench his affections towards us; being there is so much blackness with our beauty, so much deformity with our comeliness, so much corruption with our graces. No, so much blackness, and so little beauty, and so much corruption, and so little grace. But he looks upon us, not as we are in ourselves, but as we are in Christ, and not what we are for present, but what he intends to make us in Christ. He looks to the *end* of his design, even to that which he has designed us to, when we shall be presented without spot or wrinkle, or any such thing. Holy, and without blemish, (Eph. 5:27), when we shall be satisfied with his likeness, (Psalm 17:15), when we shall be like to the angels; no, like to God, glorious with his glory, as now gracious with his grace.

And therefore, God having intended us to such high purposes, and looking on us for the present, what he purposes to make us, and what he has designed us to, necessarily the heart of Jesus Christ must be taken with us.

Part 4: General Application

In this way having showed you, what it is to have the heart of Christ taken with the church; and proved to you that the heart of Christ is in this way taken with it; and given you the grounds and reasons of it; I will now descend to application.

If it is true that the heart of Jesus Christ is taken with his church and people, then from here we may deduce these various truths.

The first is that, 1. This then may be a ground for us to expect, and here our faith may be strengthened in the expectation, that Christ will yet do more for his church and people, than what he has done.

Indeed, he has done much for our nation, for our English Zion. He might have ruined us, for a generation of such as provoked him. We have been a provocation of his anger to this day. He might have suffered our carcasses to have fallen in the wilderness, and kept our posterity to have entered into Canaan. We have looked toward Egypt, toward Babylon. He might have laid the foundation of purer times in our blood, raised up a purer church on our ruins.

But God has seemed to over-look our great unworthiness. And to the terror of our enemies, and even to the astonishment and wonder of us all, has begun, set forth, and gone forward in a way of mercy; such ways as have been untrodden in former times. And that which God has given us in hand, is an earnest of what we have in hope. What we have in possession presses us to look to what we have in promise, and expect its performance, because God loves the church. The heart of Christ is taken with the church. He loves his church, and therefore, he will purify his church, and take away her dross and tin. He loves his church, and therefore will he reform his church. He loves his church, and therefore will he take away whatsoever offends, all soul-burdens, all conscience-burdens, which oppress the spirits of his own people.

1. The church is his fold, and he will destroy the wolves, which have gotten in to devour the sheep. 2. The church is his field, and he will weed out the tares, and bind them in bundles to burn them. 3. The church is his house, and he will sweep it. 4. It is his floor, and he will fan, and blow away the chaff. That love which made him engage himself to his church, in precious promises, will not suffer him to rest, until he has made good those promises to it. That love which moved him to begin, will not suffer him to rest, until he has made an end.

You see in Ezekiel 37:27, the whole chapter is but an addition of mercy to mercy. When God begins to go forth towards a people, in a way of mercy, he knows no stop, he can make no end. I will do this, and also this, as you see in that chapter. God adds mercy, to mercy. And the reason is, because free-love begins, and that knows no end.

The proceedings of God's mercy, towards his church and people, do arise from himself, his own free-grace. His justice is from us; but his mercy is from himself. If, when he threatened to punish Israel, he said, he will "add judgement to judgement." This, and this also will I do, (Amos 4:12). How much more then when he promises to show mercy to Israel, will he add mercy to mercy? God has also of mercy, as well as of judgement. See it in Ezek. 37:27, "My tabernacle also shall be, *etc.*

Well then is the heart of Christ taken with his church and people? Then will we with confidence believe, and with patience wait and expect, that Christ will yet do more for his church and people, than ever he has done, because he loves them?

Let us but join supplication with expectation; praying, with waiting, and we shall see it, to the joy of our hearts. I never read, that God ever bestowed any great mercy and deliverance on his church and people, but he first stirred up the hearts of his people mightily to pray to him. And never did God mightily stir up the hearts of his people to seek him, but he fashioned some great mercy and deliverance for them. God loves to make his people as thankful as they were prayerful, as happy enjoyers, as they were humble seekers. When trouble sends us to prayer, then deliverance shall send us to praises. Let us then join our supplications to our expectations. Times of great expectations, should be times of great supplications. Whether they are 1. Expectations of hope, the object of which is good. 2. Or, expectations of fear, the object of which is evil. 3. Or, mixed expectations between hope and fear, as our times are; they are times of expectation, and therefore they ought to be times of supplication. We are now big with expectation; let us now be mighty in supplication. Great stones are not to be turned over without great strength. Great mercies are not to be gotten without great strivings. The man-child of deliverance is not to be brought forth without pangs. Let us then be mighty in prayer. That will make all our present difficulties subservient to deliverance. And then let us stand still and wait. 1. Wait for performance of promises. 2. Wait for performance of prayers.

There are many thousands of prayers registered in God's book, and many thousands of tears put up in God's bottle. Let us wait when all these shall come down on our heads in a warm shower of mercy. Wait for when the great revenue of prayers will come in. The longer the stay, the greater will be the harvest. We say, great engines move slowly. Small things are quickly wheeled about; but great mercies are long in conception, long in the womb, and long in the birth.

This is all our comfort. God will not bring to the birth, and afterward not bring forth. Nor will he bring forth, and afterward shut the womb again, as he says in Isaiah 66:9. He is Alpha and Omega, the Beginning, and the Finisher; where he lays the foundation, there he will lay its roof.

2. If the heart of Christ is once taken with his church and people, then he will never take his heart off from them. His heart once taken, shall never be taken off.

Men may love today, and hate tomorrow. But God cannot. Whom he loves once, he loves to the end; even to all eternity. As there was nothing in us, that was the ground of his planting his love on us, so, there is nothing that shall be able to over-turn the thoughts of his love, when once they are fixed on us.

Indeed, our behavior may be such, as may cause God to be angry with us, and correct us sharply; yes, and make us to know, we had better never to have tried such things with him. But there is nothing which shall cause him to hate us, and cast us off. He may correct his spouse, but he will not divorce her. The Israelites were so hard-hearted, that for every trivial fact they would put away their wives. But the Lord hates putting away, (Mal. 2:16).

For sin fore-seen was not able to hinder him from planting his heart on us. But though he saw what we would be, yet he loved us. How then shall it be able to over-turn the thoughts of his heart, when once they are fixed on us?

Men indeed are not able to see to the utmost of things; they are not able to discover and foresee all the inconveniences and evils that may arise. And therefore, that being discovered after, which was not foreseen before, may be a ground to alter their affections, and change their thoughts, when fixed. The less judgement and for-sight in men, the more fickleness, and changeableness in men.

But now God foresaw all. He foresaw all that which you now think is a ground for him to alter his mind to you. And, if all that foreseen could not hinder him from *fixing* his love on you, neither shall it be able to move him to *take off* his heart, when once his heart is taken with you.

Here, he is said to make an everlasting covenant with us, and he will never depart from us. No, he will put his fear into our hearts, that we shall never depart from him, (Jer. 32:40).

And Isa. 54:9-10, "Saith the Lord (speaking of the covenant of grace, which he will make with his people) It shall be as the waters of Noah unto me. For as I have sworn that the waters of Noah should no more go over the earth. So have I sworn that I will not be wroth with thee, nor rebuke thee." As if he had said, this is as sure as the other. The one as firm as the other. You have experience of the one, believe the other. I give you the same pawn, the same seal of heaven to confirm it.

If men were as bad as devils, they will by their works never bring a second flood on the world, because God has sworn never to destroy it. And as he has sworn to that, and is therefore, steadfast and immutable. So he has sworn to the other, that he will never leave you, nor forsake you; and therefore God will not.

Objection. But alas! Do we not see that God sometimes forsakes his church and people?

Answer. Now for the answer of this, we will premise these three distinctions. 1. There is a seeming, and there is a real forsaking. 2. There is a temporary, and an eternal forsaking. 3. There is a partial, and a total forsaking.

From these we will lay down three conclusions, in answer to the objection.

1. Conclusion. God sometimes seemingly, when he does not really forsake his people. God does not really neglect his people, when he seems to neglect them. He seemed to neglect and forsake Job, Heman, David, Christ himself, when he cries, "My God! My God! Why hast thou forsaken me?" It was *dissimulatio, non indignatio*, as one speaks. He feigned himself to be gone, but was not gone. The cloud may take the sun from our sight; but not pull it out of the sky. God may seemingly be gone, when he is really there. He seemed to be gone from Job, but he was really there. Otherwise Job could not have trusted in him, in that great difficulty.

The same I may say of Heman, of David. Though God seemed to be gone, yet he was really there. Otherwise they could not have prayed, exercised their faith, and sought after God, as they did.

So also was it with the church in the Song of Songs 3:1 and chapter 5. And that is the first conclusion, God may seemingly forsake his people, when not really forsake his people.

2. Conclusion. God may partially forsake his people; but he never totally forsakes them. I say, God may in part forsake his people, which may be occasioned on their part, by some fresh and new-acted sin. As you

see it was with David, Psalm 51:1. David had sinned. God had withdrawn himself. God was gone, comfort was gone, light was gone for a time. Works of darkness, and walking in darkness went together. He did not follow the direction, and therefore lacked the consolation of the Spirit. But though God does this partially sometimes, yet he never totally forsakes his people.

For the clearer understanding of this conclusion, you must know there is a threefold presence of God, 1. Quickening. 2. Comforting. 3. Supporting.

1. God may forsake a man in part, in respect of his quickening presence, and leave a man to the barrenness, flatness, deadness of his own spirit for a time, that the soul cannot pray, hear, meditate, do anything, as formerly it has done. As it was with Samson when his locks were cut, his strength was gone; and therefore, though he thought to go out, and do as he did in former times, yet he found there was no such matter; he had become even as another man. So it is here; our strength lies, not in our hair, but in our head. When God is gone, our locks are cut, our strength is gone. And though we may think to go on doing duties, as at other times, and meet with those lively and vigorous workings of Spirit in duty, yet, we shall find no such matter; we are even become as other men.

Indeed, so much of his quickening Spirit God leaves in the worst of times, as usually, to keep up the heart to duty. The soul will pray, will read, *etc.* But he gives not so much, as to carry the soul through the duty, with that life and vigor of affection, which formerly it had.

There was a time when the soul never came to prayer without an inflamed heart, never on the duty, without a quick and enlarged soul. But now the spirit is dead in duty, cold in duty, heartless in the performance of those things, in which the heart was so much taken.

2. God may forsake a man in respect of his comforting presence. Though man is not able to rob us of our comforts, and take away our joys, they are such as the arms of men are not long enough to reach; yet God can. He may eclipse our joys, and dampen our comforts, and withdraw the beams of his countenance from us, and leave us in darkness and trouble. I say, he may turn our day into night, our light into darkness, our comforts into discomforts.

You see, it was in this way with Job, with David, with Heman, Psalm 88. Who, although they had the quickening-presence of God, yet they lacked his comforting-presence?

And indeed, of the two, it is better to lack the comforting, than the quickening-presence. Better to lack comfort than life, joys than graces, or their lively exercise. The one is the essence (*esse*), the other but for the good (*bene esse*) of a Christian. A man may live, and serve God, and obey him; and yet lack his comforting-presence; as you see, Isa. 50:10.[6] But he cannot live without his quickening-presence.

3. God may forsake a man in part, in respect of his quickening-presence, and he may more forsake a man in respect of his comforting-presence. But God does never forsake us in respect of his supporting-presence.

In the saddest condition, in the darkest night, in the stormiest day, the soul has still support from him. David, Job, Heman, they lacked the comforting-presence of God for a time; but yet they had his quickening, and they had his supporting presence.

As he told Paul, so he did for all. His strength was seen in their weakness, and his grace was sufficient for them. Sufficient to bear them up in the trial, and sufficient to bring them out of the trial. So much for the second conclusion.

3. Conclusion. God may forsake his people for a time, but not forever. It is but a temporary, not a final, not an eternal forsaking, Isa. 54:7-10, "For a moment have I forsaken thee; but with everlasting kindness will I gather thee, have mercy on thee. For the mountains shall depart, and the hills shall be removed. But my kindness shall not depart from thee."

And in this way these points shall serve for the answer of the objection. And notwithstanding that, the conclusion is firm. That if the heart of Christ is once

---

[6] "Who is among you that feareth the LORD, that obeyeth the voice of his servant, that walketh in darkness, and hath no light? let him trust in the name of the LORD, and stay upon his God." (Isa. 50:10).

taken with his church and people, he will never take it off; he will never completely forsake them.

And, as God will not forsake his church, as forsaking has relation to spiritual cases, and soul-distresses, so I might show you at large, to prevent another objection. That he will not forsake his church, as forsaking has relation to temporal and outward distresses. You may take his word for it, Joshua 1:5, "I will not leave, nor forsake thee." It is true, it was a promise made to Joshua in particular; but belongs to the whole church of God in general. General promises may have particular applications, and particular general.

As general promises belong to every particular member, so particular promises may belong to the whole body. And therefore, though it was a promise to Joshua, yet the apostle (who knew the mind of God) makes it ours, as well as his. He brings it into the common-stock, and shows it part of our riches, Heb. 13:5, "Let your conversation be without covetousness; for he has said, he will never leave thee, nor forsake thee." In brief; he will not forsake his church: 1. Either he will protect them from danger. 2. Or he will deliver them out. 3. Or he will support them in. 4. Or he will sanctify everything to them.

And this is the third conclusion which flows from this doctrine. 3. If the heart of Jesus Christ is taken with his church. Then all the passages of God's providence in the world, are for the good of his church and people. All the dealings of God in the world, not a step God takes in the world, but he walks towards his people in it.

1. All the passages of God's providence to the church in general.

2. All the passages of God's providence to any member of the church in particular, they are all for good.

1. For the first, all the passages of God's providence to his church in general, they are for good. Are they sad, or are they joyful, they are all for good. Are they sad? It is to humble them, to quicken them, to purge them, to purify them, to blow away their chaff. This is certain. Whatever is done in the world, is done either by God's permission, or by God's commendation. God must either permit, or allow of whatever is done in the world. And assure yourselves, God would never permit, much less would he ever allow, and approve of anything to be done in the world, which should not be for the good of those he loves so dearly.

Whatever way the wind blows, be it north, or south, good or evil, all is for the church's benefit. As theevil, and destructive to the good and comfort of his church and people.

Here it is, that Christ turns the saddest and sorest perplexities that ever the world shall see, into an use of comfort to his church. Luke 21:25-28, "There shall be signs in the sun; and moon, and stars, distress of nations, with perplexity," *etc.* Men's hearts failing them for fear, and for looking after those things which are coming on the world; for the powers of heaven shall be shaken; and then shall they see the Son of Man coming in a cloud, with power and great glory. When these things begin to come to pass — then look up, and lift up your heads. "For your redemption draweth nigh."

One would think this were a strange consequence deduced from such an antecedent. A consequence so comfortable, from an antecedent so terrible. It seems strange, that such a terrible doctrine as this, should afford a use of consolation. Yet, it is so. No matter what the premises are what they will, the conclusion is good. If his providences are what they will, his promises are good. And those promises shall turn all his providences *to good* at last.

2. As all the passages of God's providence to the church in general, so every passage of his providence to any member of it in particular, is for the good of the church.

1. All your enjoyments, they are love. You may read the heart of Christ, the image of a friend, engraved on all you have. You may behold the impress of love, the good will of God circled about all you do enjoy.

All that wicked men do enjoy, is but from the hand of God; that is the highest tenure they can show; even his general providence, which causes the sun to shine upon the good and bad, and this tenure may be cut off at pleasure.

Part 4: General Application

But all that you do enjoy, is from the heart and good will of God. They are expressions of his good will to you, and you may read love in all. No, they are the earnests of further love. You may see and read heaven and glory in all you have.

Part 5: Particular Application

We may well say; whatever the people of God do enjoy, they are: 1. The fruits of prayer. 2. The performance of promises. 3. Expressions of love. 4. Encouragements to believe. 5. Enablements to obey. 6. Earnest pennies of heaven and glory.

All your needs, as well as all your enjoyments are mercy, are love. There is an expedience in all the sad passages of God's providence to you. They are expedient to try you, expedient to humble you, to exercise you, to win you, to wean you, *etc.* Whatever your condition is, it proceeds, 1. from God who is the best of beings. 2. From the best of God; his heart and good will. 3. It is the best for you.

Wicked men have a curse hid in their best things. A curse in their gold, a curse in their silver, a curse in their health. But God's people have a blessing hid in the worst things. You have a blessing in poverty, a blessing in sickness, a blessing in crosses, a blessing in death itself.

Riches are not in the promise, but mercy is in the promise. Though poverty, yet mercy; though afflictions, yet mercy; and you can all tell me, a cross in mercy, is better than a comfort in wrath. A loss in love, better than an enjoyment in displeasure. More die in the flood, than in the ebb. Though prosperity is more cordial, yet afflictions are more physical. We often go and drink an excessive amount of cordials, when medicine alone does us good. And a sanctified cross is better than an unsanctified comfort, *etc.*

4. If the heart of Christ is taken with his church and people: 1. Then see what a fearful thing sin is, which causes God oftentimes to deal harshly with that, which his soul loves so dearly. God oftentimes afflicts and punishes his church sharply and severely. Which yet his heart is much taken with. And sin is the cause. And therefore, what a fearful thing is sin! How grievous would it be to you, to be forced to take hard courses with a child your heart is taken with? Though it is to do him good.

Why, God is taken with his church, and do you not think it moves God to afflict and chastise it? We would gladly do all the good we can to the people we love. O! We can never do enough for them. Why, so it is with God to his church. He loves his church, and willingly would he do anything for it. And it is the grief of his soul, that he must take contrary courses with us, to do us good. That he must be forced to afflict and chastise them he loves so dearly. To bring them to life by death, to good by evil, to a crown by crosses.

When God parted with the ten tribes, you see what a conflict there was in him. How his bowels stirred, and were moved towards them, notwithstanding all their sins, Hosea 11:8, "How shall I give thee up, Ephraim! How shall I deliver thee, Israel! How shall I make thee as Admah! How shall I set thee as Zeboim! My heart is turned within me; my repentings are kindled together." How loath was God to seal to a bill of divorce! His heart loved her, though she was an adulteress to him.

And when Judah justified the sin of her sister Israel, exceeding her in idols, what trouble was it to God to cast her off! How willing was he to receive her after all her adulteries? Jer. 3:1, "Thou hast plaid the harlot," *etc.* And when she would go on in her adulteries: yet how unwilling still was he to give her up? Until at last it grew so high, that there was no remedy, (2 Chron. 36:16). He must necessarily do it.

And when he had done it, how exceedingly was God's heart moved, that he must be forced to deal so hardly with them he loved so dearly? Read Jer. 12:7-9, *etc.* See how God laments over the loss of that which their sins would not give him leave to keep. "I have forsaken mine house! I have left mine heritage! I have given the dearly beloved of my soul into the hand of her enemies!" And what was it that forced God to deal so hardly with them he loved so dearly? Why it was sin, (2 Chron. 36:15-16). He sent messengers, because he had compassion on them. They mocked the messengers of God, and despised his words, and misused his prophets; until the wrath of the Lord arose against his people, until there was no remedy. And which of these has remained to be done among us? How has our sun been darkened; the stars lost their light! How many burning and shining lights have been taken out of our candlesticks, and planted in others! How many blown out by the rage of wicked men!

Did we not justly fear, by reason of that idolatry, superstition, profanation of sabbaths, persecution of the saints, and messengers of God, that our day was gone; our night approaching?

Did we not fear, that we were come up to this, that there was no remedy? That God should have opened the sluices of his wrath, and let in a sea of his displeasure on us? Made us a field of blood, long before this?

Ah, my brethren! Never nation, never church from whom God has showed himself more unwilling to depart and leave, than England. Look on the passages of us to God, and his ways towards us; and see how unwilling he declared himself. God has upheld us, as if he himself should fall, if we did not stand. As if his glory could not stand, if we fall. As if his glory had depended on our preservation.

And how can we better answer God's dealings towards us, than to abandon that, cast out that which was our fear, and gave God just occasion to destroy us? Let us now do by our sins as the Israelites did by their leaven. There was 1. *Inquisitio fermenti.* There was search made for it. So let us search out that leaven of sin, superstition, idolatry, which have soured our kingdom, and laid us open to the stroke of God's wrath. Search your houses, search the land, search your hearts.

2. Ejectio fermenti. 3. Execratio fermenti. And let all be found in us, if ever we would have a Passover.

Otherwise our preservations from former, will be but reservations to future, and worser evils. Sin will cause God to punish those he loves.

5. If the heart of Christ is so much taken with his church, then let this show you, into what way you resolve to your heart all the passages of God's love to his church and people, even into his own love. His grace is the rise, and his glory is the end.

There are two main streams, in which the goodness of God runs to his church. 1. The higher, and 2. The lower. But both of these streams have the same head, the same spring from where they come, even his own love. 1. For the higher, or upper streams, and these are four. 1. Election. 2. Justification. 3. Sanctification. 4. Glorification. And all these arise from the great abyss, and sea of his mercy toward his church.

His heart is taken with us; and therefore, 1. He chose us, Deut. 7:7-8, "The Lord loved you not, nor chose you, because ye were more in number than any people. But because the Lord loved you." So, God did not set his heart on us, because we were better than others; for there are others in the world who might have been made more lovely.

His heart is taken with us; therefore, 2. He justifies us. We could do nothing to strike off any former score. For all we did, set us further in debt: it was but an adding of sin to sin, guilt to guilt. The sin of our righteousness, to the sin of our unrighteousness, covering a blot with a blot, as Isa. 30:1.

No, it did arise from this. His heart was taken with us, therefore did he justify us. Titus 3:7, "We are justified freely by his grace." The same is found in Romans 3:24, 4:5, which show, that into this, all the expressions of his love are resolved.

His heart is taken with us; therefore, 3. He did sanctify us. Our holiness is not fashioned out of our own principles; spun out of our own bowels; compassed by our own strength and industry, but freely imparted and given of God.

As our righteousness is freely imputed, so our holiness is freely imparted. That you are not a killing Cain, a self-murdering Saul, a despairing Judas, a profane Esau, a drunken Baltazar, a filthy sodomite, it arises from this, mere mercy.

But that God has not only restrained you, but renewed you; not only chained up your spirit, but changed your spirit. This is free-mercy. And so, the scripture tells us, 1 Peter 1:3, "Blessed be the God and Father of our Lord Jesus Christ, who of his abundant mercy has begotten us again — not only mercy, but abundance of mercy. So, James 1:18, "...of his own free-will begot he us." And that in John 1:13, "We were born again, not of blood, nor of the will of the flesh, nor of the will of man, but of God." Not of blood, nor great men, nor good men can do it. Regeneration does not come by generation. Nor of the will of the flesh, our will is but a fleshly will, and cannot beget a spiritual nature. Nor of the will of man, it is not all the endeavors of holy men, who labor to do us good, that can do it. But the will of God, it is a mercy we give least concurrence to, of all other. When we have grace, then we are helpers for the growth, and increase of grace. But who shall give grace?

When the candle is lit, it will burn; but none but God can light up the candle. After sanctification we concur. There is no concurrence in regeneration. This is the freest mercy of all other. When God has fashioned grace, there is some engagement for God to go on. But there is nothing to move him to bestow grace. Here is the ground. His heart is taken; therefore, he sanctifies us.

His heart is taken with us; therefore, 4. He glorifies us. As our justification, so our sanctification, and glorification arise from the same ground. His heart is taken with us.

The papists indeed would have us to merit heaven. And the Roman Catholic *Council of Trent* denounces a curse on those, who say, a justified person cannot merit heaven. But alas! What are all our deserts to this glory! If a man should serve God, and suffer a thousand years, what were this to merit eternity in glory?

No, here is the ground of everything. His heart is taken with us, and therefore, he glorifies us. And so, the scripture speaks plainly. Eph. 2:5, "By grace ye are saved." And lest he should never make it firm enough, he adds, in the 8th and 9th verses, by grace ye are saved ... not of works.

So that you see into what to resolve the higher streams of his love. His choosing us, his justifying, his sanctifying, and his glorifying us. His heart is taken with us — therefore, he chose us; therefore, he justifies us, *etc.*

2. As you may see into what to resolve all the higher. So, the lower streams of his love to his church. All into this. His heart is taken with his church. His heart is taken with us; therefore, he protects us. His heart is taken with us; therefore, he will preserve us. His heart is taken with us; therefore, he will support us. His heart is taken with us; therefore, he will deliver us.

All the good we have in hand, and all the good we have in hope. All the mercies bestowed, and all those which God is bestowing on us. Look upon all as a continued thread spun out of the bowels of free-grace, and mercy.

God has done great things for us; and from this they have arisen. His heart is taken with us, his love towards us, Jer. 31:3-4, "I loved thee with an everlasting love; — therefore with loving-kindness have I drawn thee."

Alas! If God had looked on us, and taken either ground or motive from anything in us, to do this for us, we should never have enjoyed it.

1. There was no ground, no foundation of desert in us, (we abhorred its thoughts), for God to raise such a fabric of mercy on, as he has done.

If anything in his church were the foundation of the structure of mercy, which we expect God to raise, we might look for a mean building. Such weak foundations must have as weak a structure. A building must be proportionable to the foundation. But seeing God's own heart is the foundation; his own mercy and good will towards us, which is so strong, so firm, so full a foundation. Therefore, it is, that we may expect a structure of mercy suitable to the foundation.

And, as this is the foundation of all those great and stupendous things, which God has done for us. So, it is a ground for us to expect, that God will yet do greater things for us, than ever he has done.

Indeed, when we look on ourselves, we are at an end in our thoughts, and think God is at an end in his mercy. But when we look up toward God, and see there the ground of what we have, this keeps up our hearts from sinking, and causes us to look on all we have, as an earnest of more.

Men that are at the top of a high place, if they look downwards, their eyes dazzle, and their heads grow dizzy. But if they look up towards heaven, they recover themselves again. God has raised us up to some height of mercy; and if we look downwards, if we look on ourselves, we are driven past the utmost of our thoughts. But let us look up to heaven, where this mercy we have, has its spring and foundation, and we shall quickly recover.

Though there is nothing in us, yet there is something in God; and that which is in God is the ground of this mercy, and therefore will he go on in the ways of his own mercy.

I have often thought within myself; how far God at this time has out-done his people in mercy. He has not only out-done the deservings of his people, but out-done the desires of his people, the prayers of his people. And consulting below, I am ready to think God is at an end of his mercy.

But, when I recover myself, and look on the ground of God's doing good to his church and people, not to be any goodness in the church, but merely his own goodness, this revives me again; he puts a *heart* into me (and understanding) that God will yet do greater things for his church, than yet he has done.

As I said before; when God executes judgements on his church, he adds judgement to judgement. So much more, when he comes in a way of mercy to his church, he adds mercy to mercy.

God is oftentimes weary in going on in a way of judgement, because the exercise of his judgements are drawn out by us, by our sins. He is said not to afflict willingly. And his judgements he calls his strange work. It is not so natural to God, and therefore he is quickly weary of it.

But God is never weary of the exercise of his mercy; and therefore, he goes on to add mercy to mercy. We say, the bee gives honey naturally; the sting only, when she is forced to it. So, God, it is natural to him to show mercy, but he is provoked to exercise judgement.

Here he is called the Father of mercies, begets mercy. Mercy is the issue of God, most natural to God; and being so, here mercy pleases him. Actions of nature are actions of delight. God is never so well pleased with any carriage towards his church, as those which are in the ways of mercy.

No, if he afflicts his church, it is to show mercy. Mercy is the end of all his dealings towards his church; and therefore, mercy being so natural, so pleasing; and that the mercy of God is the ground of his expressions of love to us, as it is. Though our sins may draw out the expressions of his justice; yet his mercy arises from himself. Here we may have a ground to expect yet greater things than ever.

6. If the heart of Christ is so much taken with his church. Then see with what confidence we may pray for the good of the church of Christ. Christ's heart is taken with it.

A man may pray for himself, and doubt of hearing, because he is not able to make out his particular interest in God's love. But if a man prays for the good of the church, he is sure to have hearing, because the heart of Christ is taken with it.

Let us then make use of all our interest and acquaintance in heaven, in the behalf of the church at this time. 1. It is a thing, which God commands. 2. A thing, which God expects. 3. A thing, which God rewards. 4. A thing, which God threatens the neglect of.

Much might be said to move you. Your good, and your evil lies in the churches. As Jeremiah used this as an argument, why, to pray for the civil estate of Babylon; because in its peace they should have peace. If theirs is gained in Babylon, how much more ours in Zion?

7. If the heart of Christ is so much taken with his church, then what will become of those, who are enemies to his church and people! Is the heart of Christ so much taken with his church and people, then woe be to them that offend his church! If you touch them, you touch the apple of his eye.

God's people are dear to God. They are his spouse, his children, his members, purchased with the price of his blood; his inheritance, his portion, all his comings-in. Those he died for, shed his blood for, one drop of this is worth a thousand worlds. And therefore, those whom he was content to shed his blood for, certainly he more esteems than all the world besides.

We say, while the iron is in its own nature, you may handle it, and meddle with it; but if once the nature of fire is added to it, if you touch it, it will burn you. So while the children of God, are but the children of men, you may deal with them as with other men; but if once the nature of God is stamped on them, the image of Christ is drawn on them, it will be dangerous for you to meddle with them, lest fire break out of their mouth to devour you.

We read in Zech. 12:3, God said, he would make his church "a burdensome stone," *etc.* St. Jerome on that place says, it was a metaphor taken from the custom of the Jews, who to try their strength, had at the gates of the city great stones; if they could lift them, well and good; but if not, they crushed themselves with them. So, God will make his church a burdensome stone. Whoever lifts it, shall crush himself; whoever seeks to hurt it, shall ruin himself. You see it in Pharaoh, Haman, Ahithophel, Julian.

Haman lifted so long at this stone, that it fell on him at last, and crushed him.

Pharaoh followed the children of Israel so long, that he could not return at last, but was overwhelmed in the waters.

Julian attempted it so long, until at last he himself was overthrown.

He that shoots in a weapon that is over-charged, strikes down himself, and does not hit that which he aimed at. He who intends evil against the church, shoots in a piece over-charged, and is sure to be struck down with his own recoil.

We see it in our days. They who have dug pits for us, have fallen into them themselves. They who laid snares for us, in them is their own foot taken. They have but made rods for their own backs; paved a way to their own destruction; dug graves to bury themselves, in seeking our ruin.

The scepter of Christ has been too strong for the principality of Satan, he has a rod of iron; a scepter of power, an arm of strength, to crush in pieces all his enemies. And therefore, as Pilate's wife said of Christ, "have nothing to do with that just man." So, I say to you, do you see a godly man? Beware of having anything to do with him, by way of offence. For their angels always behold the face of their heavenly Father.

8. If the heart of Christ is so much taken with his church, then see here the ground of acceptation of the services of his people.

God being taken with the persons, is taken with the performances of his people. He had respect to Abel, and then to his offering. Christ, his heart, was taken with the person, and then with his performance.

Here Christ says to his church, Song of Songs 2:14, "Let me see thy countenance, let me hear thy voice. For thy countenance is comely, and thy voice is sweet." Indeed, if acceptation should arise from the worthiness of our duties, we should never look to be accepted. There is so much sin in our services, so much evil in our good, so much coldness in our best works, so much formality in our chiefest power, so much deadness in our best life, so much of the world, so much of our earth in our employments for heaven. And if acceptation should arise from any worth in them, we should be sure to miss it. But arising from his good will and mercy to us, his heart being first taken with us, is taken with our performances. Here is the assurance of being accepted.

No, and not only of our purest and most perfect services; but even of our poor and imperfect duties, such as we throw away for dead, and cast prayers, Song 5:1,

"He drinks the milk as well as the wine." We look upon a prayer accompanied with deadness, distraction, as a cast prayer. O! we say, how can God accept of such impure, imperfect services!

But here it does not arise from the excellency of your prayers, but from the indulgency of his grace. It is the voice of his spouse, though never so weak. It is the cry of a member of his, though never so faint. And he can put his odors, his incense to them, though never so impure, and make them acceptable, (Rev. 8:4).

Part 6: Use of Examination

But now, my brethren, it will be a great matter of inquiry, whether we have an interest in this love, as one said when he looked on the rainbow, and in that read God's covenant, never to drown the world again. Ah! But he says, what is this to me, if I am drowned. I may be drowned, though the world is not drowned. So, you might say or think this, "You tell us of the exceeding love of Christ to his church. But what if I am not of his church? What if I have no interest in his love? What is all this to me?"

But then I suppose you are desirous to know whether you have an interest in this love. It concerns your everlasting good to have an interest, and your present comfort to know you have an interest.

Now in this inquiry I would have you, 1. To examine your hearts thoroughly. Deceits lie low. A false evidence is the fruit of a slight and superficial search.

2. In your inquiry do not let anything which is compatible with any, who have no interest in this love, be a foundation on which your soul rests.

I have told you sometimes, and tell you again, whatever another man may have and do, and yet have no interest in this love of Christ, cannot be a sufficient evidence for you, that you having or doing that, have an interest. Acquaint yourself with the most clearing and proving evidences.

3. Take your evidences from the carriage of the Spirit, neither at the best, nor at the worst, but the middle way, which is mostly who you are.

If you look on yourself at the worst, you may be discouraged. If at the best, you may be deceived. Many have had such affections in a heat or fervor of spirit, which in cold blood have nothing of them.

4. Do not judge yourself by particular actions and carriages. But look on the universal frame and bent of your spirit. No certain rule is to be established on a particular instance, whether good or bad.

I might lay down other rules to observe in your inquiry. But we will come to the inquiry itself.

Would you know whether you are one with whom Christ's heart is taken? See whether you are of his church. Are you one, who are taken out of the world? Are you one, whom God has called? One whom he has justified? One whom he has regenerated? Sanctified? Are you one, who are washed, purged, renewed? These might be general ideas, and may be considered too obscure. But I will name you but one, and it is a plain one, and there is nothing more demonstrative than this.

Would you know whether the heart of Christ is taken with you? Why then see, are you one, whose heart is taken with Christ? If Christ is taken with you, you are taken with Christ. It is a mutual, a reciprocal taking. Whatever God does to the soul, it makes an impression in the soul of the same to God. God delights in us, and on this we come to delight in him. God knows us, and on this we know him, (John 10:14). God apprehends us, and on this we apprehend him. He chooses us, and on this we choose him. He loves us, and on this we love him, (1 John 4:19). His heart is taken with us, and on this our hearts come to be taken with him. Our love to him is nothing else but *radius amoris dei erga nos in deum reflexus,* a beam of God's love reflected back on God. So that this now is a true character of Christ's heart being taken with you, if your heart is taken with Christ.

Question: But you will say, how shall I know whether my heart is taken with Christ?

Answer. For the answer of this, because on this foundation I will lay the whole weight of this discourse, in this use, 1. A heart taken with Christ, is a heart which knows Christ, and has tasted of Christ. Are you such as know Christ? For knowledge of Christ precedes the love of Christ. He who does not know, cannot love. Things unseen may be loved, but things *unknown* cannot be loved. 1 Peter 1:8, "Whom having not seen ye love," but never not known.

All love to Christ arises from discoveries and manifestations of Christ to the soul. Either from the discoveries of those beauties, those attractive excellencies that are in him, or with that, from the discovery of his heart and good will towards us.

Now blind men cannot discern of beauties; nor ignorant men of the beauties of Christ. Christ is to them as a mine of gold covered over with earth and rubbish, as a bed of pearl and diamonds hid with a heap of sand. He is as a glorious Messiah under a contemptible outside, and men have lacking eyes to see through the veil of his flesh. Through the bark and outside of his humanity, they can behold no beauty in him, as Isaiah speaks of carnal men, (Isa. 53:2). When you behold him, you see no beauty in him, that shall make him desired.

Now then, are you one who knows Christ? Did God ever reveal him to you in a promise? What visions has Christ made to your soul? What manifestations? What discoveries that may evidence to you, that you know him?

There are four manifestations, or discoveries of Christ to the soul, which do exceedingly take the soul. Indeed, every vision of Christ takes the heart. But at these times the heart is not only wooed and won, but overcome with his sweetness and glory.

1. After the soul has long lied bedridden in sorrow, been overwhelmed in the deeps of legal humiliation, and have been broken and shattered in pieces with consternation, and apprehensions of sin, and God's wrath for it, then a discovery of Christ, and vision of Christ to the soul, is a resurrection from the dead.

When Christ comes by a promise into the soul, and displays his glory, the riches, and greatness, and freeness of his grace, as to Moses, "the Lord God, gracious and merciful, long-suffering, and abundant in goodness and truth, keeping mercy for thousands, forgiving iniquity, and transgression and sin," (Exod.

34:6). "I, I am he who forgiveth thy iniquities, *etc.* (Isa. 43:25). Then is the soul beyond expression, enamored with him; now it is overcome with his beauties and excellencies, and even ravished with his love. And this is the first eminent taking of the heart with Christ.

2. When the soul has been on the stormy sea of temptations and desertions; has long labored under the sense of God's withdrawings and absence from the soul, and Christ returns again, breaking the dark and thick cloud, and shining into the soul. Who can then express the warmth, the comfort, the revivings, the holy heats and flames of love and affection to Christ?

You see how it was with Job. "I have heard of thee with the hearing of the ear. But now mine eyes see thee." And certainly, the sight of God's beauties took him. Those eyes which saw him were like a burning-glass to the heart, to kindle the flames and fervors of holy affections towards him again.

You see how it was with the church in Song of Songs 3:4. Christ had withdrawn himself. She makes inquiry after him, but could not hear of him. At last after all her trouble, Christ appears to her soul. And you may read there, how exceedingly her heart was taken with his return. "I found him whom my soul loveth; I held him, and would not let him go, until I had brought him into my mother's house."

3. When the soul sits down to contemplate, and read over the beauties and loves of Christ, when it is in the contemplations of those surpassing excellencies, and

admired sweetness which is in Christ, and Christ (while the soul is busy in feeding on these thoughts) makes a discovery of himself to the soul. Makes the soul to see a vision of his glory. O! How is the heart taken with him! It is even drowned and sunk in a sea of glory. Ah! What clasping, what embraces! What loves are there then between Christ and the soul! It is impossible for me to express this, or for me, or you to conceive. It is a vision of glory, the porch of heaven.

4. When the soul is under outward pressures, afflictions, prison, sickness, on one's death-bed, then a visit of Christ, a discovery of himself exceedingly ravishes and takes the heart. Here is kindness indeed, riches for the poor, liberty for a prisoner, a cordial for the sick; here is all in Christ's manifestation.

Well then, would you know whether your heart is taken with Christ? Do you know Christ? Did you ever see the face of Christ in a promise? What manifestations has Christ made to you? What manifestations within you in the work of grace? What manifestations to you in the beginning of glory? You who do not know Christ, cannot love Christ.

1. Sign; a heart taken with Christ, is not excessively taken with anything else.

The sweetness of Christ overcomes all the sweetness in other things, in the creatures. As it is nothing but ignorance which makes men admire anything here on earth, if men knew the excellence of other things, they could not admire such trifles as they do. So here, it is nothing but ignorance of better things which makes us dote on things here below. Did we see his beauties, all the world would be blackness. Did we see his fulness, all the world were but emptiness. I say, did we but know the excellencies and beauties of Christ, and the satisfying-sweetness of his love, nothing should have a room in our hearts, except he alone. The higher we ascend toward heaven, the lesser will the things on earth appear. If you go to the top of the mountains, men would appear but small. But if it were possible to go up to the sun, the mountains would appear as nothing.

The love of Christ has a raising-power, working our hearts as high as heaven, and being there, all things here below are of no account and esteem to the soul. So, Paul says that very thing about a man on fire with the love of Christ. "Yea doubtless I count all but loss for the excellency of the knowledge of Christ — and do count them but dung, that I may win Christ," (Phil. 3:8).

Well then, they whose hearts are taken with the creature, taken with the world, taken with sin and vanity, these are too gross to be taken with spiritual loves.

2. Another sign. What the heart is taken with, the soul seems to live more in it, than in itself. Do but examine it in anything the heart is taken with, whether your comforts, your delights, your happiness, whether it does not lie in them. The worldling, he lives in his possessions. The voluptuous man in his pleasures. And can no more live out of them, than the fish out of the

water, the salamander out of fire. So here, if your heart is taken with Christ, then you live more in Christ, than you do in yourself. "I live, yet not I, but Christ," the apostle says (Gal. 2:20). You cannot any more subsist without him, than the beam without the sun, or the spark without the fire. No, no more live without him, than the body without meat, no, the body without the soul. Christ is to the soul, as the soul is to the body. Now, as the body cannot live without the soul, so the soul cannot live but in Christ, who is *anima animae*, the soul of the soul, "for me to live is Christ."

I say, if your heart is taken with Christ, you live in Christ more than in yourself. Your life, your comforts, your happiness, they are all folded up in him, as Judah said of Benjamin. Jacob's life was bound up in the lad's life, Gen. 44:30, so the soul of Christ says, my life, my joys, my comforts, they are all bound up in my church. "All my fresh springs are in thee," God says of his church, (Psalm 87:7). "And, whom have I in heaven but thee! And in earth in comparison of thee!" (Psalm 73:25), says the enamored soul of God, his heart was taken with God, and he lived in God more than in himself.

It was the speech of Luther, who (being in a great distress and spiritual trouble) had written about the walls and table in his study, in great letters, *vivit.* A friend comes to him, and demands the reason. He replies, *vivit Christus; & si non, non optarem unam horam vivere,* — his life was in Christ. He lived more in Christ than in himself.

This makes the life of a Christian so safe, none can hurt him, and so sweet too, being a life in Christ out of himself. The best of others lies in themselves. But the best of a Christian, those precious things in him, lies out of himself, and lies in Christ.

3. Sign. What the heart is taken with, that the comforts of the life are upheld by from day to day. We have many a weary step to go, and can no more go without comfort, than Elijah without food. Comfort is to the soul, as the soul is to the body. As the body without the soul is dead, so is the soul of men without comfort.

Now, would you know what your heart is taken with, then, see what the comfort of your life is upheld by from day to day. Is Jesus Christ the comfort of your life? Is he the joy of your hearts? Wicked men have a variety of springs. If one is dry, they go to another. But the saints have but one: Christ. And if he is gone, all is gone.

4. Sign. A heart taken with Christ that has high apprehensions and valuations of Christ. It values and esteems him above all the comforts and contentments in heaven and earth. Psalm 73:25, "Whom have I in heaven, but thee! And in the earth, in comparison of thee!" Here is the breathing of a soul taken with Christ. He prizes Christ above all the comforts and contents in the world.

For the better unfolding of this sign, there is, 1. Something considerable in the act. 2. Something in the object — Christ is prized. 3. Something in the measure — above all the comforts, contents, *etc.*

1. In the act of prizing Christ, we do not mean a bare and naked estimate of Christ, in the understanding. But such an one as prevails with the soul, and commands the spirit of a man to do actions consonant and agreeable to that rate the judgement set on Christ. I say, by prizing Christ, we do not mean a bare act of adjudication, what a man in his judgement may conclude Christ to be worth. Many are they that will tell you, they conclude Christ to be worth a world, who yet will not part with anything for Christ.

But I mean such an act of the understanding, as brings up the heart, and the affections to close with Christ in that height which the understanding rates him at. I say, such an act of apprehension as prevails with a man to do actions consonant and agreeable to the rate it pretends to set on Christ, as in the case of the wise merchant. He did not barely judge that the pearl was worth all he had. But he did actions consonant and agreeable to it. Seeing he could not enjoy the pearl without parting with all he had to compass it, he sells all to gain the pearl.

That is the first. A soul taken with Christ not only barely judges and esteems Christ worth everything, but will part with everything to gain the Christ.

2. Here is something considerable in the object. Christ prized.

1. We do not restrain and limit this only to the person of Christ. There is something in the person of Christ, which may prevail with an unbeliever, to esteem

him. The dignity of his person being God-man, having all beauties and excellencies in him. This may raise up a kind of esteem of Christ in the hearts of unbelievers.

2. Neither do we limit it only to the benefits of Christ, and the great things which he has done for man in general, in his humiliation, death, passion, *etc.*

But we are to take Christ in the extent of Christ: Christ in his whole latitude. Christ in his holiness, Christ in his laws, Christ in his government, Christ in his truth, *totum Christi,* the whole of Christ. He that does not prize Christ in his whole latitude and extent, does not prize Christ at all as he ought to do.

As we say of faith; it does not *eligere objectum*, choose its object, single out what it will esteem, and what not. But prizes of Christ fully in the latitude and extent of Christ, of Christ in his person, Christ in his beauties, Christ in his laws, in his holiness, truth, government. Many desire Christ as Savior, without ever acknowledging Christ as King. The soul taken with Christ is taken with all of Christ, as he is lovely in all things. So, the soul loves everything about him and prizes and esteems all of Christ.

3. That which is considerable in the measure is, that a soul taken with Christ, prizes Christ above all comforts and contentments in heaven and earth.

This Christ commands, Matthew 16:24, "If any man will come after me, let him deny himself." He says "if any" it is set down indefinitely. Not only you, who are poor, and have little to lose, and deny yourselves in. But they, who have most. You that are rich, you that have lands, possessions, have crowns and scepters. If any poor, any rich, any beggar, any prince, *etc.* "He must deny himself," not only in things unlawful, but lawful. He must yield up his sins as a snare, his comforts, estate, and everything as a sacrifice for Christ, if he calls for them. Matthew 10:37, "He that loves father or mother more than me, is not worthy of me." These relations are expressed. But under these are comprised all the comforts and contentments of the earth.

And this was not only commanded, but it is practiced by those, whose hearts are taken with Christ. You see in Abraham, who left all; in Moses, who prized more of the reproach of Christ, than all the treasures in Egypt; in David, Psalm 73:25, "Whom have I in heaven but thee! Or in earth, in comparison of thee!" As the world would be nothing else but *angiae stabulum,* a noisome sink, a prison to a godly man, were it not that he enjoys something of Christ here. So, heaven itself were but a gaudy pageant, vanity, if God and Christ were not there.

The heaven, which carnal men imagine is a Turkish-heaven, a heaven of pleasures, delights, comforts, but *fleshly and outward.* They conceive of it, according to their principle.

But the heaven of a godly man, it lies in God, it lies in Christ. Indeed, that is not heaven, which is *merely near to* God; but that is heaven, which lies in God, to a godly man.

It was the meditation of one, "Not heaven, O Lord; but God, and Christ, for I would rather have ten thousand times Christ without heaven, than heaven without Christ."

In this way the soul that is taken with Christ, prizes Christ above all the comforts, contentments of heaven and earth.

5. Sign. A heart taken with Christ, the thoughts are taken up with Christ. Such a man thinks about Christ, and he speaks Christ, he *lives* Christ. You know whatever a man's heart is taken with, it is never off his thoughts, never off his heart, he is never well but thinking and speaking of that which he loves. The thoughts are the character of what the heart is taken with. If your heart is taken with Christ, your thoughts are taken up with him. Christ is always on your thoughts; he lies next to your heart. When you go to bed he is with you, (Song of Songs 1:13). And when you awake, he is with you, as David says in Psalm 139:18.

Indeed, God's people may have swarms of other thoughts; but they are not entertained, they are not welcome to them; they are their burden, and trouble. They come in as intruders, and are not entertained as guests. A wicked man entertains them as guests, as friends; but they come into a godly man, as intruders, never invited, nor find they are welcome. This is that which Jeremiah speaks. "How long shall vain thoughts lodge within thee?" In a wicked man's heart, they are lodgers, and entertained as guests; he keeps doors open, spreads a table for them, makes them a bed, bids them welcome. But in a godly man they crowd in, and find no entertainment.

And as the thoughts are taken up with Christ, so also is the tongue taken up. He thinks, and he speaks Christ. When Christ is in the heart, the tongue will discourse and speak of him. Whatever is in the heart, and the heart is taken with, that a man's discourse is most taken up with. As Psalm 37:30, "The mouth of the righteous speaketh wisdom, and his tongue talketh of judgement." And why? "Because the law of his God is in his heart," (verse 31). So here it is on the same ground. Your talk shall be of Christ, of his beauties, his love, *etc.*, because Christ is in your heart. What the heart is taken with, the tongue will speak about.

1. And indeed we cannot have a fuller subject to discourse on. Other subjects are empty subjects, quickly barren. Talk of what you will, you will be quickly at an end. The bottom of other things are quickly sounded. But Christ is a full subject. Whatever you fall on, is fulness in Christ, an everlasting spring, which affords fresh supplies of matter, new and unconceivable discoveries arise afresh to be the matter of supply to all eternity.

2. You cannot have a sweeter subject. Christ is all-sweet; a rose without prickles. A rose, for sweetness, without prickles, for contentment. And nothing is like this but Christ. All the things of the world since the fall, have been roses beset with thorns. Though there are

many sweets in the world, yet they are not completely-sweet; they are beset with thorns. Crosses with comforts, and afflictions with affections. Christ is all-sweet, and nothing but sweet. *Tota pulchra*, as he said of his spouse, "You are all-fair." Beauty without spot. Sweet without prickles. He is a garden full of flowers, full of sweets. You can speak and consider nothing like this, but in Christ you may lay your thoughts and rest on him, and go home satisfied.

3. You cannot have a more delightful subject. Christ is the delight of all both in heaven and earth. He is God's delight; his heart is taken with him; he lies in his bosom. And his Son, in whom he is well pleased, he is the delight of the angels, whose delight it is to study Christ, and desire to learn and hear further discoveries of Christ by his church, as Peter has it in 1 Peter 1:12.

4. You cannot have a more profitable subject. A subject which in conversing on, we are transformed into his glory, (2 Cor. 3:18), into the glory of him, who is the subject of the discourse. Have you not been kindled with heavenly fire? Have your hearts not burned in the discussions of him, as well as in conversing with him? Indeed, we cannot speak about him correctly, but in some measure we converse with him.

Does it not sometimes fetch up your souls to glory, and leave you in heaven? Do you not find it profitable to quicken you? To raise you? To comfort you? To inflame you? To humble you? To melt you? To transform you? Does not a discourse of his love quicken you, when you are dead? Comfort you, when you are dejected? Raise you, when fallen? Humble you, when proud? Inflame you, when you are cold? Enlarge you, when straightened, and pent within yourselves?

O! That such worthless subjects should so often take up our tongues and thoughts! And Christ, so full, so sweet, so delightful, so profitable a subject, which shall be matter for our souls' discourse to all eternity, shall be thrown aside, as if not worth taking up!

You, whose hearts are taken with Christ, declare it to your own comfort, and the good of others. In this let your thoughts be taken up with him, let your discourses be more of him, show yourselves to love him, by thinking Christ, speaking Christ, living Christ more.

6. Sign. A heart taken with Christ, thirsts after communion with, and nearer conjunction to Christ. You know whatever your hearts are taken with, you desire, and thirst after communion, and converses with. So, it is here between Christ and the soul. The soul taken with Christ longs to be with him, and thirsts after communion with him. 1. In grace here. 2. In glory hereafter.

1. In grace here. O! How the soul once taken with Christ desires converses with him, in prayer, in hearing, in meditation. Isa. 26:8-9, "The desire of our soul is to thy name, and to the remembrance of thee. With my soul have I desired thee in the night; yea with my spirit within me will I seek the early." And this is the genius of a soul taken with Christ. That duty does not make him

content, if he does not find Christ in the duty. If the end of a duty has left him on this side Christ, it has left him so far short of comfort.

Others indeed, though they do a duty, yet as their hearts do not seek Christ in the duty, so their souls can rest content without him, when the duty is done. But it is otherwise with a born-again soul.

It was the words of John Bradford that he could never leave a duty, until he had found communion with Christ in the duty; until he had brought his heart into a duty-frame. He could not leave confession, until he had found his heart touched, broken, and humbled for sin; nor petition, until he had found his heart taken with the beauties of the things desired, and carried out after them. Nor could he leave thanksgiving, until he had found his spirit enlarged, and his soul quickened in the return of praises.

And it was the happiness of Bernard, a heaven on earth, that he said of himself, "I never went from you Lord, without you." He found God in every duty. He had communion with God in every prayer; which indeed is heaven on this side heaven.

In this way he, whose heart is taken with Christ, thirsts after communion with him, and no duty makes him content in which he has not found either his quickening, or his comforting presence. Either communion with his grace, or communion with his comfort.

2. As he thirsts after communion with him here in grace, so he desires communion with him in glory, to be with the Lord, as the apostle says. While the soul is here, it sees the distance too great between Christ and it, that she cannot enjoy that sweet communion with him. As the apostle says, "While we are present in the flesh, we are absent from the Lord." And therefore, the soul breaths after him, desires to be with him. *Cupio dissolvi*, the apostle says, "I desire to be dissolved, and to be with Christ."

The same is said of David. Psalm 42:1-2, "As the hart panteth after the water-brooks; so panteth my soul after thee, O God. My soul thirsteth for God, for the living God. When shall I come and appear before God!" He had tasted the sweetness of Christ, and did not fear the bitterness of death. He had life in patience; death in desire; because by death he should be carried to more sweet and intimate conjunction with Christ.

It was the thought of Augustine, "Lord, I will die, that I may enjoy thee. I will not live, but I will die. I desire to die, that I may see Christ; and refuse to live, that I may live with Christ."

And this disposition you see in the spouse here in the Song. Her heart being taken with Christ, she could not brook the distance between Christ and her; and therefore, cries out, Song of Songs 8:1 "Make haste, make haste my beloved."

The more the soul believes, and the more the heart is taken with Christ, the greater are the desires to be with him. Until Simeon had gotten Christ into his arms, he was unwilling to die. But after he had Christ in his arms, "Lord, now lettest thy servant depart in peace; for my eyes have seen thy salvation."

Indeed, here are but the espousals between Christ and the soul. Some broken-rings, contracts, espousals, between Christ and us. But then is the great marriage-day, the solemnization of our nuptials, to all eternity.

Here we do see him but dimly and darkly, at the best, and there are oftentimes clouds come in, and interpose themselves, between Christ and us. But then we shall see him face to face, and never shall any clouds come between Christ and us to all eternity. There we shall see him in his glory, his full discoveries.

Here we enjoy him but in part. The distance is great between him and us. All which distance arises from that within us. Were it not for sin we might be in glory, even in grace. But at that time we shall enjoy him in *fulness*.

Heaven is the place, which God has intended to set forth himself to his people in his glory, to all eternity. Heaven is where there shall be no fears, no sin, never a hint of distrustful thoughts shall arise anymore. Where there shall be no sorrow, no tears. All sighing and sobbing shall pass away, and nothing but joy shall keep the house. "We are now the sons of God. But it doth not yet appear what we shall be; for we shall see him as he is."

7. Sign. A heart taken with Christ thinks nothing too much to do, nothing too much to suffer for Christ. You know love cannot be posed. We say, there is no difficulty in love. Things impossible to others, are easy to them who love. And things burdensome to others, are delightful to them who love. If once your heart is taken with Christ, you will think nothing too much to do, nothing too much to suffer for him.

As Christ thought nothing too much for us, because his heart was taken with us; neither shall we think anything too much for Christ.

We read how prodigal the saints have been of their riches, their blood, their lives for Christ, because they loved him. 1. They have not accounted their estates too dear for him, Heb. 10:34, "They took joyfully the spoiling of their goods."

2. They have not accounted their lives too dear, Rev. 12:11, "They loved not their lives to death for him." If they must dig in mines, or be cast to be devoured by wild-beasts for Christ, as it was the usual sentence of Christians in the primitive times, they were willing to do and suffer it.

See this in the virgin of whom Basil speaks, who was condemned to death, because she would not worship idols. And the same of old Polycarp and others who were martyred.

This is certain, a soul taken with Christ knows no difficulty in its love. It loves him with an unlimited, an uncircumscribed love, which no duty, no difficulty can pose.

8. Sign. A heart taken with Christ is exceedingly cast down with the withdrawings and absence of Christ. The comforts of the soul are laid up in Christ. And when he is gone, all is gone. Comfort gone, joy gone, the heart gone with him. As Mephibosheth said, "take all, now my Lord is come back." So the soul says, take everything, take the world, take riches, take heaven, and glory, so far as heaven and you are concerned, this is important, that my Lord may return to my soul. Darkness is terrible to the soul, and this is thick darkness, and therefore one says with Absalom, "let me see his face," *mea non prosunt sine te*, "nothing besides thee, can either satisfy or profit me."

9. Sign. A heart taken with Christ is fully content and satisfied with the enjoyments and possession of Christ. The possession of the thing loved contents the soul so far as there is satisfaction and contentment with it. The reason why we do not meet with full contentment and satisfaction here in the possession of our loves, is because they lack fulness.

But now it is not so with Christ. He is able to brim the soul, to satisfy the spirit, to answer all the desires of the heart; and therefore, the heart taken with him, must necessarily rest satisfied and contented with him.

Such a gulf of desire is in the soul of men, that if God should cast in a thousand worlds, there would be no contentment, except Christ is cast in too. And Christ is so full of contentment, that if God bestows him, they will neither need nor desire anything more.

And in this way, we see this serves for our use of trial and examination. We will now come to a use of exhortation, and conclude this.

Part 7: Use of Exhortation

I bring an exhortation, 1. To them of Christ's church. And, 2. To them who are not of the church.

1. To them of his church. Is it so that the heart of Christ is so much taken with his church and people? 1. Walk suitably to this love. Dignities, and suitable walkings to dignities must go together. Now this suitable walking we will express in these five things. 1. Walk cheerfully. 2. Walk thankfully. 3. Walk humbly. 4. Walk watchfully. 5. Walk obediently.

1. Walk cheerfully. Walk as heirs of such a mercy. Here is a truth that speaks comfort, when all the world speaks nothing but terror.

Beware of abusing this love. Precious things are committed to us by a word of caution. This is a precious truth; and therefore, let me add to it this word of caution. Beware of abusing this love of Christ.

Christ's love are his inner affections, and he will never endure to have his inward affections injured, his love abused. You know a man will not have his love injured; the abuse of his power, of his wisdom, greatness, does not touch a man so nearly as the abuse of his love. This is an injury which men cannot endure.

So, to speak after the manner of men; Christ can least endure his love should be abused. There is no abuse like it. Therefore, beware of it.

A Treatise of the Loves of Christ to His Spouse

Now, this love of Christ is injured these ways, and beware, 1. When we slight the entreaties, reject the tenders, cast aside the offers and beseeches of his love.

When love stoops to you, when the mercy and goodness of Christ does as it were, come on its knees to you, and intreats you to do this, or not to do that, and yet you will stop your ears, pull back your shoulder, slight the entreaties, this is an abuse.

2. When the love of Christ slackens our hearts to duty, loosens our engagements, makes us more remiss to or in service. This is to abuse his love.

We should reason from mercy to duty; and not from mercy to liberty. Abundance of grace calls in for abundance of duty. The love of Christ should constrain us; as the apostle says, (2 Cor. 5).

This should make us live more humbly, more actively, more studious to please, more diligent to obey, more careful to serve him. This should make us live at higher rates for heaven, more spiritual, more heavenly minded. It is a cord let down from heaven, to fetch our souls up there. And does this cause us to be more remiss, more careless? Does this, which should quicken, slacken our hand to duty? O! this is a base, ungrateful neglect of his love!

3. When we take heart to sin by it. Grow more loose, careless. This is a high abuse of this love. Because God is good, will you be evil? Because he is merciful, will you be sinful? Because he is gracious will you be impious? What fearful abuse of love is this! This is to

wound Christ in the house of his friends, to return good for good, is but human. To return evil for good, is wicked. To return good for evil, is Christian-like. But to return evil for good, and the greatest evil for the greatest good, sin for love, this is devilish.

Were you his enemies, he knew how to deal with you; he could revenge himself, and the abuses of his love on you. But you are his friends, and those affections which you wrong, are stirred in him, when he goes about to punish you. "Oh Ephraim! How shall I give thee up! How shall I deliver thee, Israel! My bowels are turned within me. My repentings are kindled together," (Hosea 11:8).

The greatness of God prevails with wicked men; that awes them often, that they do not dare sin against him. But the goodness of God; this should prevail with us, "there is mercy with thee; therefore you are to be feared." It is set down as the principle in such, with whom the heart of Christ is taken, (see Hosea chapter 3). "They shall fear the Lord, and his goodness, in the latter days."

None but venomous spirits will suck poison from such sweetness, as there to draw encouragements to sin from that which is the great encouragement to be in service of Christ.

The love of Christ had so prevailed with Chrysostom, that he used to say, *ego sic censeo, sic assidue praedicabo.*[7] And Anselm, that if on the one hand

---

[7] *I believe I am so loved, so insistently that I praise him.*

he should see sin, and on the other, the torments of hell, he had rather choose to fall into hell, than fall into sin.

4. When we stagger and doubt, give way to misgiving thoughts of Christ's love, and unbelief of our own hearts, we abuse this love.

What, is it possible that Christ should do or suffer more than he has done and suffered to persuade your hearts of his love? If Christ should ask the question of you, who doubt most of his love, "What shall I do to answer your scruples. To satisfy your souls forever, in this, that I love you?" Could you rationally desire more than what he has expressed in his words, and to your heart, and if notwithstanding everything is in vain? May he not justly say as David of Nabal, "Surely in vain have I done all this, when this all cometh to nothing."

3. Be much in the contemplation of this love of Christ. Dwell on this. This love of Christ will be a matter of eternal perusal in heaven. We shall do nothing but read over this love. O! Let us not be strangers to it now.

View it in the 1. Fulness. 2. Freeness. 3. Bounty. 4. Perpetuity of it.

1. Measure it in its fulness. It is a love which reaches to every necessity. A love able to make you holy, and able to make you happy. You are under guilt and sin; you are terrified by the one, and ashamed and confounded because you are so loathsomely defiled by the other. Why? It is a pardoning, a purging, a sanctifying love; it is a love as large as himself, though the persons beloved are finite.

2. Read it over in its freeness. 1. It was undeserved, and 2. It was an unsought-for love.

1. It was an undeserved love. We may provoke him to anger, but we cannot tempt him to love. The former arises from our sins, the latter from himself. His choosing, justifying, adopting, saving love, all are free.

2. It was an unsought-for love. Never a prayer put up for it. "I am found of them that sought me not," (Isa. 65:1).

3. Read it over in the bounty and expressions of it. 1. What he did. 2. What he suffered. 3. What he has given to his church. 4. Look upon it, in its perpetuity, permanency, and continuance. It is a love which reaches from eternity to eternity. From eternal choosing, to eternal glorifying. An unchangeable love.

Let us then peruse this love. Read it over in all the dimensions. Dwell on its thoughts until your hearts are humbled, melted, enabled, ennobled, won, quickened, comforted, *etc.*

The thoughts of this love are, 1. Soul-humbling thoughts. Nothing lays the soul lower than love. The consideration of this will loathe a person in their own thoughts, (Ezek. 36:25-33), where we find some expressions of love, how it affects us to humble us.

These would be, 2. Soul-melting thoughts. They will not only humble, but melt; not only break, but dissolve the heart. Nothing melts the soul more than love.

The law may break us; but it is as the breaking of a flint; every piece of dust retains hardness. But it is the gospel that melts us. The thoughts of God's justice make the heart stony, make it harder. But the thoughts of God's mercy melt the heart.

You know you never mourn indeed, until love, until mercy melts you. Every drop of tears sticks like a hailstone, and congeals in the eyes. But when love comes in, then all the springs are opened, and a man is dissolved into waters.

So much apprehensions of this love of Christ. So much godly sorrow. They are like the fountain and the stream, of which the one rises no higher than the other.

The thoughts of this love have, 3. A soul-enabling power. It will not only engage us to service; (as the apostle says, "The love of Christ constrains me"), but it will enable us to service; make us pray, and pray with affections, pray with life; make us hear, and hear with strength. This puts us on working, and puts life, virtue and vigor into our actions.

There are no actions stronger than those that come from love. Things incredible and impossible to others, are yet easy to them who love.

See what the saints have gone through, what they have done, what they have suffered. Let but the thoughts of this love lie on your spirits a little, and you will find that love is strong as death, (Song of Songs 8:6). And will mightily carry us through that, which otherwise may seem impossible.

They will be, 4. Soul-ennobling thoughts. They will make you like themselves. Whatever the soul feeds on, the soul is digested into its nature. So here, feed on the thoughts of this love, and your spirit will be digested into it. While we behold through these eyeglasses the glory of the Lord, we are changed into the same image, from glory to glory, even as by the Spirit of the Lord, (2 Cor. 3:18).

In nature the meat is digested into the nature of the eater. Here the eater is turned into the nature of the meat. The contemplation of his glory makes you glorious.

They will be, 5. Soul-winning thoughts. Love, you, know is of an attractive nature. Nothing wins more than love. Love is the loadstone to draw love again.

As the sun shining on a glass creates a reflection of the beams back again, so the love of God shed abroad in our hearts, creates a reflection of love back again toward God. You see Mary. Much was forgiven her; she had tasted of much love from God; and she returned much love again to him. She loved much. The power of God shakes the heart. The majesty of God brings dread to the heart. The justice of God makes the heart to look in awe. But it is the mercy of God, the love of God, which persuades, wins, and draws the heart. Nothing wins a man's heart to God but his love.

The fear of God, dread of God, may bring a man's feet into God's ways. But it is the love of God, which brings his heart into his ways.

They are, 6. Soul-quickening and 7. Soul-comforting thoughts. Oh then! That we were but wise to improve this doctrine, this truth, to the good of our souls!

I tell the Christian, if you would give this truth but room in your heart, it would help you, and relieve you of all the burdens under which you groan.

1. Do you labor under a proud heart? This would humble you.

2. Do you labor under a dejected heart? This would raise you.

3. Under a dark heart? This would comfort, revive you.

4. Under a dead heart? This would quicken you, and put the Spirit of heaven into you, while you are on earth.

5. Under a hard heart? This would break you. No this would melt you, dissolve you into waters.

I say, the more you get up (with Elijah) into this chariot of love, the more would the mantle of sin and corruption depart from you.

6. Under a worldly heart? This would kill your heart forever to the world, and set you all aflame with the fire of heavenly affections.

I am confident of it; whatever a Christian desires to enjoy, whatever a Christian desires to be rid of, if he can but dwell on this truth, and be able to manage it, he shall have it more fully, he shall have it more quickly than any other way.

Would you be rid of a proud heart? Would you have a humble heart? Would you be rid of a dead heart, and desire a quick heart? Would you be rid of a hard heart, and have a broken heart? Would you be rid of an unbelieving, of a doubting, of a dejected heart, and would you be mighty in faith, full of comfort? Then let your soul be carried captive with this truth. Be content that this truth should master you; be willing to entertain it, believe it and embrace it. I am confident on it, so that all this will be done, I will set down the manner in which we may be wise to manage this truth!

There are many who look on this but as a pleasant dream, a fiction. And some believe it, but slightly; there lack depth in them. And there are some (poor souls!) to whom the comfort of this truth belongs, who thinks this is news that is too good for them. They think, if they should own it, it would be but too great a sale for too small a boat; rather overturn them, than do them good; rather ruin them, than help them. And therefore, they must feed on hard and dark thoughts, black thoughts, on hell, on justice, on sin, on their corruptions.

Ah! Poor souls! Satan deludes you; you take a way which will undo yourselves. Either to discourage you, to say there is no hope; or else to break you, that you shall never be able to do God service.

Look as long as you will into hell. Pry as long as you will into the dark vaults of your souls. Rake as long as you will into the kennel of your hearts. You shall find nothing in hell but hell, in your hearts nothing but sin; and having found it, you will run from him.

That man who looks too much on sin, who shuts his eyes from a mutual interview of love between God and his soul, it is here that you must come at last. Free-grace must be owned; free-mercy must be acknowledged, and advanced by you; if ever you would be saved; if ever you would be comforted.

You may think what you will; but I am very sure, 1. There are no Christians more cheerful. 2. None are more thankful. 3. None are more humble. 4. None are more believing. 5. None are more active. 6. None are more courageous. 7. None more serviceable and useful toward God and men, than they, who lie continually at the breast of the promise of God's free-grace; and own that good which God makes out to them.

You may be a Christian, but you will be a sad Christian, an uncomfortable Christian, a dark Christian, a deserted Christian, a dead Christian, an unserviceable Christian, if you go on to feed on black thoughts; and will not own that comfort which Christ tenders. If you do not embrace that good which Christ speaks, and believe the riches of his grace and mercy to poor sinners, it will not be so well with you.

Do but sit down, and from the sight and sense of your own unworthiness, take but occasion to advance free-grace and mercy. Let there be place for that to come in. Let those thoughts find entertainment, and you shall quickly find a strange change in your spirit.

Part 7: Use of Exhortation

1. You, who could not mourn before, shall now be able to pour out tears, as if you were all turned to water.

2. You, who before could not believe, could not be comforted, will even think it a wonder, that your heart should be so dark, and so doubtful.

3. You, who before were dead, shalt now find a Spirit of life come into you, and make you active in the work of the Lord.

Make an experiment of it, and you will converse more with the promise, with the love of Christ, with the free-grace of God, while you live, if you would but remove your unbelief.

But who shall remove this stone? God alone must do it. But if this were done, this truth would let in a flood of mercy on you, and even sink and overwhelm you in a sea of mercy and glory. You droop and hang down your heads, because you will not own that portion, which Christ has left you; nor that comfort which Christ tenders and speaks to you.

I give a direction to 4. Them of the church. Labor for a reciprocal affection, a mutual taking between Christ and us. Is Christ's heart taken with you? O! Let your hearts be taken with him. Does Christ love you? O! Do you love Christ? Are you dear? Are you precious to him? Let him be dear and precious to you.

Whatever God does to the soul, it makes an impression in the soul of the same to God. He loves us, and on this we love him; so his heart is taken with us, and on this our hearts are taken with him. You see here the mutual endearments between Christ and his church, "His mouth is most sweet: yea, he is altogether lovely. This is my beloved, and this is my friend, O daughters of Jerusalem," (Song of Songs 5:16).

Paul's heart was so much taken with Christ, that he was ever in his thoughts, ever on his tongue. He names him sixteen, or seventeen several times in one chapter, (1 Cor. 1:1), as Chrysostom makes note. Peter did but let a word of Christ fall, and it is a door to open to further discourse of him. He takes occasion on naming him, to enter into discourse concerning him. As you see, in 1 Peter 1:7-8.[8] So greatly were their hearts taken with Christ, that they could think nothing but Christ, speak nothing but Christ. No sentence complete, in which Christ was not part of it. He was the one of their esteems; the one of their affections; the one of their desires; the one of their delights, and so he ought to be ours.

Get your hearts taken with Christ, this will make you Christians indeed; this will make you humble, active, cheerful Christians. A heart taken with Christ is heaven on this side of heaven. A heaven on earth. Glory in clay. It is the paradise, where Christ delights to walk. It is the house, where Christ delights to dwell. It is the

---

[8] "That the trial of your faith, being much more precious than of gold that perisheth, though it be tried with fire, might be found unto praise and honour and glory at the appearing of Jesus Christ: Whom having not seen, ye love; in whom, though now ye see him not, yet believing, ye rejoice with joy unspeakable and full of glory," (1 Peter 1:7-8).

throne, where Christ sits in his glory. It is the habitation of the blessed Spirit. It is the delight of all the blessed Trinity. A heart taken with Christ is the humble soul indeed, is the active soul, the living soul, which breathes forth nothing but love and desire after Christ. It is a heart dead to the world; for the world can never take that heart which once is taken with Christ. All is empty to him, whom fulness fills. All is blackness where beauty shines.

O! Then get but a heart taken with him, and you will live a life of glory, and a life of grace. This earth, this place, is the porch of glory, the suburbs of heaven. I told you before, there were four special times in which the heart was taken with Christ. I might add a fifth, which I hope is worthy to consider in our times. When Christ goes forth in his glory, for the redemption and deliverance of his church, and punishment of his enemies, then is the heart taken with him. 1. Taken with his wisdom. 2. With his justice. 3. With his power. 4. With his mercy and goodness. Which are the visible attributes Christ manifests in the deliverance of his church. You see this in Isa. 25:9, when God went forth in his glory, to deliver his church, the saints were taken with him, even to admiration, and speak glorying. "Lo, this is our God, we have waited for him, and he will save us. This is the Lord; we have waited, and will be glad in his salvation."

Here was a triumphant song of the church. This is our God; this who appears so glorious, so full of majesty. This, this is our God, not yours. And there is good reason for this. 1. Christ never appears in his glory to his church; but he makes his church glorious.

You see, when God delivered his church from Babylon, he appeared in his glory. Psalm 102:16, "When the Lord shall build up Zion, he shall appear in his glory."

And you see, as he appeared in his glory, so he made the church glorious, Isa. 54:11-13, (speaking of the same time), "Behold I will lay thy stones with fair colours, and lay thy foundations with sapphires. I will make thy windows of agates, and thy gates of carbuncles, and all thy borders of pleasant stones."

2. Christ now comes in, with the performance of promises; and he necessarily must be glorious, and the church taken with him.

If Christ were so glorious, when he made those promises. What is he, when he comes in to make good those promises? Christ has reserved abundance of his visible glory to be seen by his church; now at the end of the world.

Our fore-fathers have seen him but an obscured Christ, a persecuted and kept-down Christ. Though glorious, yet humble-glory. But it will not be long before the church sees him in all his glory, when he comes to destroy that man of sin with the brightness of his coming.

Blessed be God for what our eyes see. Let us follow him with admiration with the church. This is our

Part 7: Use of Exhortation

God; follow with spiritual triumph. This is our God. And let our hearts be taken with his goings forth; who is set forth in his glory now to redeem, and to deliver his church and people.

FINIS

Other Helpful Works Published by Puritan Publications

The Guard of the Tree of Life, a Discourse on the Sacraments
by Samuel Bolton (1606-1654)

When you participate in any ordinance of God, you draw near to him, or you offend him. Samuel Bolton shows that drawing near to God should be a solemn and holy act each time the Christian partakes of the sacrament of the Lord's Supper. A rare treatise by a Westminster Divine.

The Christian's Deliverance by Christ and the Nature of Practical Religion
by John Kettlewell (1653–1695)

This work on Practical Religion, which centers on the Gospel of Jesus Christ, was Kettlewell's first work ever published, and was eminently popular. It takes basic Christian doctrine and makes it exceptionally practical.

Taking Hold of Eternal Life in Christ
by George Gifford (1547-1620)

Is holiness of life a necessary prerequisite for getting into heaven? Do you have the power as a Christian to overcome sin? What has Jesus Christ done in enabling you to live righteously according to his commandments? How do you successfully glorify Jesus Christ in your daily walk?

Part 7: Use of Exhortation

The Victorious Christian Soldier in Christ's Army
by Urian Oakes (1631–1681)

Are you an over-comer? Have you ever been successful in conquering the remaining sin of the old man? Are you engaged in spiritual warfare every day for the good of your soul and glory of the Christ?

A Call to Delaying Sinners
by Thomas Doolittle (1632–1707)

This work really needs no introduction; it would be enough just letting Rev. Doolittle loose on your soul. It is a puritan gem. Puritan evangelism at its best!

Captives Bound in Chains Made Free by Christ
by Thomas Doolittle (1632–1707)

This is a potent and biblical treatment of being freed from sin and bondage through the blood of Christ. Doolittle is like a drill that drills into the conscience of the reader. This is a wonderful book on Christ's redemption for both the believer and unregenerate to come and drink from Christ.

Resisting the Devil with a Steadfast Faith
by George Gifford (1547-1620)

In consideration of spiritual warfare, Gifford directs the reader to resist the devil's assaults and submit before God with the weapon of steadfast faith.

www.ingramcontent.com/pod-product-compliance
Lightning Source LLC
Chambersburg PA
CBHW070205100426
42743CB00013B/3051